Josiah Tucker

**An humble address and earnest appeal to those respectable personages in Great-Britain and Ireland, who, by their great and permanent interest in landed property, their liberal education, elevated rank, and enlarged views, are the ablest to judge**

Josiah Tucker

**An humble address and earnest appeal to those respectable personages in Great-Britain and Ireland, who, by their great and permanent interest in landed property, their liberal education, elevated rank, and enlarged views, are the ablest to judge**

ISBN/EAN: 9783337306090

Printed in Europe, USA, Canada, Australia, Japan

Cover: Foto ©Andreas Hilbeck / pixelio.de

More available books at **www.hansebooks.com**

A N

# HUMBLE ADDRESS

A N D

# EARNEST APPEAL

T O

## THOSE RESPECTABLE PERSONAGES IN GREAT-BRITAIN AND IRELAND,

W H O,

BY THEIR GREAT AND PERMANENT INTEREST IN LANDED PROPERTY,

THEIR LIBERAL EDUCATION, ELEVATED RANK, AND ENLARGED VIEWS,

ARE THE ABLEST TO JUDGE, AND THE FITTEST TO DECIDE,

W H E T H E R  A

CONNECTION WITH, OR A SEPARATION FROM

T H E

## CONTINENTAL COLONIES OF AMERICA,

BE MOST FOR THE NATIONAL ADVANTAGE, AND THE LASTING BENEFIT OF THESE KINGDOMS.

---

*Suis et ipsa Roma viribus ruit.*     HOR.

---

SECOND EDITION, CORRECTED.

---

## BY JOSIAH TUCKER, D. D.
### DEAN OF GLOCESTER.

PRINTED BY R. RAIKES;
A N D  S O L D  B Y
T. CADELL, IN THE STRAND, LONDON,
M. DCC. LXXV.
[PRICE ONE SHILLING AND SIXPENCE.]

AN

# HUMBLE ADDRESS, &c.

My Lords and Gentlemen,

THOUGH the Author of the enfuing Tract may be below your Notice, as an Individual, yet the Subject he treats upon, highly deferves your moft ferious Attention. In the prefent unhappy Difputes between the Parent-State and the Colonies, he undertakes to point out, what Meafures the Landed-Intereft of *Great-Britain* and *Ireland* ought to purfue in future, for the Sake of themfelves and their Pofterity. And if what he has to offer, fhould, after a due Examination, be found to be reafonable, folid, and fatisfactory, he relies fo much on your own good Senfe and Judgment, as to believe, that you will not reject his Plan, merely becaufe it originated from an inferior Hand. This is all the Favour he afks, or expects from you.

A 2

Upon

Upon this Subject, he waves the Considera-
tion of every Thing, which might have a Tendency to keep the present Question out of
Sight. *Great-Britain* and her Colonies are now
at open War. This is the Fact. But if it
should be asked, How these Things came to
pass? From what Causes did they spring?
Which are the real, and which are the apparent
Motives in this Controversy? Moreover, who
were originally and principally to blame? And
what Methods ought to have been taken at first,
in order to have prevented Matters from coming to their present Height?---The Author having already given his Sentiments on each of
these Heads in his 3d, 4th, and 5th preceding
Tracts, and also in his Letter to Mr. Burke,
will not here repeat the same Things.---The
grand Object now before him is simply this;
*Great-Britain and her Colonies are at open War*:
And the proper and important Question arising
from such a Fact is the following, *What is to be
done at the present Crisis?*

Three Schemes have been proposed;---the
Parliamentary,—Mr. Burke's,—and my own.

The Parliamentary Scheme is,—To maintain *vi et armis* the Supremacy of the Mother-
Country over her Colonies, in as full and ample
a Manner, as over any Part of the *British* Dominions.

Mr.

MR. BURKE's is, [tho' not in exprefs *Words*] To refign or relinquifh the Power of the *Britifh* Parliament over the Colonies, and to erect each Provincial Affembly into an independent *American* Parliament;---fubject neverthelefs to the King of *Great Britain*, with his ufual Prerogatives:---For which Favour of acknowledging the fame Sovereign, the Colonifts are to be complimented with the moft precious Rights, Privileges, and Advantages of *Britifh* Subjects:---I fay, *complimented*, and complimented even *gratuitoufly*:---For as to their contributing any Proportion, either of Men or Money, towards the public Expence, and in Return for thofe Favours:---All this is to be entirely left to their own innate Goodnefs and Generofity, to do juft as they pleafe.

MY Scheme [which Mr. BURKE, in his laft Speech of *March* 22, 1775, is pleafed to term a *childifh* one] is,---To feparate totally from the Colonies, and to reject them from being Fellow-Members, and joint Partakers with us in the Privileges and Advantages of the *Britifh* Empire, becaufe they refufe to fubmit to the Authority and Jurifdiction of the *Britifh* Legiflature:---Offering at the fame Time to enter into Alliances of Friendfhip, and Treaties of Commerce with them, as with any other fovereign, independent States.

Now

Now, in order to determine, which of thefe
Schemes is the moft eligible;---it would be
right to confider, which is the eafieft and moft
practicable,---which is leaft expenfive,---which
is likelieft to prevent fimilar Difturbances and
Difputes for the future,---and which will leaft
endanger the *Englifh* Conftitution and our do-
meftic Tranquility. For all thefe Circumftances
ought to be taken into the Account, before a
due Judgment can be formed.

In regard to the firft, I wifh for the prefent
to be filent about it;---partly out of Refpect to
that auguft Body which has given a Sanction to
it;---partly becaufe it is now upon Trial, whether it can be executed or not;---and partly likewife becaufe this muft fall of Courfe, if either
Mr. Burke's, or mine, fhould be judged to have
the Preference. For thefe Reafons, I fay, I wifh
to keep a refpectful Silence on this Head.

But in refpect to Mr. Burke, I need not
ftand on fo much Ceremony. For tho' he is
confeffedly a great *Rhetorician*, and can with his
magic Voice raife a mighty Tempeft of meta-
phorical Lightenings and Thunders;---yet,
Heaven be praifed, there is the Period of all his
Powers: And his *verba ardentia*, his *flaming
Words*, are found to end at laft (like many
other Explofions) in Noife and Smoke. Nor
doth it, I humbly apprehend, follow, that the

Orator

Orator is endowed with a greater Portion of political Difcernment than other Men, or with more difinterefted Sincerity, and real Love of his Country, in making a juft and honeft Application of that Difcernment;—merely becaufe he has more Words at Command, and can mufter up a greater Army of bright Similes, and florid Expreffions.

But be that as it may:— I now confider myfelf as ftanding at the Bar of the public Tribunal: And therefore before the Jury is ftruck, and the Trial begins, I humbly beg Leave to claim, and to exercife one of the diftinguifhing Privileges of *Englifhmen* in fuch Cafes, viz. To except againft all fuch Perfons in the Pannel, who appear to be under a wrong Biafs, and an undue Influence refpecting the Nature of this Difpute.

And 1ft. I except againft *Courtiers and Placemen*, confidered *as fuch*. This is not uttered out of a Spirit of Refentment, Pique, or Difappointment, according to the Mode of modern Times. For, I thank God, I have no Caufe to complain of any Difappointment; having fince my Advancement to the Deanery of *Glocefter* in the Year 1758, neither directly, nor indirectly made the leaft or the moft diftant Application for any other or higher Station. This Renunciation of afpiring Views is a Circumftance, which I am perfuaded Mr. Burke knew perfectly well, by various Means, and from different
rent

rent Perfons, efpecially from a noble Lord,
formerly high in Office, and a great *Favourite* at Court, but now his Coadjutor, and
a flaming Patriot. And yet the Orator has
been pleafed to characterize me by Name in
his Speech of the 19th of *April*, 1774, without any Provocation, as one of thofe *Court-
Vermin* (fuch was his polite Phrafe) who would
do any Thing for the Sake of a Bifhoprick.---
Moreover I do not make this Exception againft
Courtiers from any bad Opinion I have conceiv-
ed of the prefent Set of Minifters: For I think
it may be fairly allowed, without paying them
any Compliment, that they are to the full as *able*,
and as *honeft* as the beft of thofe who are endeavouring to fupplant them. But neverthelefs, as
they are fubject to many unhappy Biaffes, which
may draw their Judgments afide without finifter
Intentions, they ought to be excepted againft in
the prefent Difpute. In fact, while the great
Continent of *North-America* fhall continue to
be united to this Ifland under any Mode whatever, Perfons in Adminiftration will neceffarily
have a Multitude of Places and Sine-cures to
difpofe of, many lucrative Contracts to beftow;
and to fpeak in coarfe, tho' very expreffive
*Englifh*, many Jobs of various Kinds, where-
with to gratify their Friends, and Dependents.
Not to mention, that if ever a total Separation
(fuch as propofed by my Plan) fhould enfue,
the

the Miniftry for the Time being, would run a great Rifque of falling a Sacrifice to the blind Zeal of popular Difcontents, and the knavifh Intrigues of Party-Factions. Therefore for all thefe Reafons, I muft infift, that Courtiers and Placemen ought to be excepted againft, as being not fufficiently unbiaffed, or difinterefted to determine impartially on the prefent Subject.

2dly. I particularly except againft the whole Band of Mock-Patriots. And my Reafon is, becaufe this Race of Men will of Courfe, prefer that Scheme, whatever it be, which can furnifh them with the moft lafting Fund for Oppofition and Complaint. Now it is evident, that our Conjunction with *North-America*, upon any Terms, and under any, or every Modification, will not fail of becoming an inexhauftible Source of Altercation and Reproach, let whatever Meafures be purfued. For Example : had the Miniftry propofed at firft that very Scheme, which Mr. BURKE has now thought proper to recommend, the Heads of the Faction, and even Mr. BURKE himfelf (if he had not been a Penfioner to *North-America*) would moft probably have propofed juft the Reverfe ; that is, they and he would have infifted on the Neceffity of *obliging* the Colonies to contribute a Share, *proportionably to their Intereft, and to the growing Benefits they receive*, towards the maintenance, the Grandeur, and the Glory of that Empire, from which their

B                                             own

own Prefervation and Profperity are derived.
And then the popular Cry would have been,
that a wicked and a profligate Adminiftration
were going to facrifice the Honour and Dignity
of the *Britifh* Crown, and the dear-bought
Rights and Privileges of the *Britifh* Nation to
*American* Gold, and *American* Ingratitude. ——
Then we fhould have been told (and every Town
and Country News-Paper would have echoed and
ro-echoed the Tale) that *America* was the Property of *Great-Britain* by every poffible and legal
Claim ;---by Right of Difcovery,---Right of Oc-
cupancy,---Right of Poffeffion,---uninterrupted
Prefcription,---Communication of Benefits,---
Participation of Pofts of Honour, and Places of
Profit,---general Protection,---never-ceafing Defence, &c. &c. And then we fhould have been
told with peculiar Emphafis, that this new-
fangled, minifterial Scheme of erecting fo many
new Parliaments, all co-ordinate with each other,
under one general Monarch, was not only a no-
torious Breach of the *Englifh* Conftitution, and
utterly repugnant to the Law of the Land ;—
but was alfo a deep-laid, diabolical Contrivance
to fubjugate thefe petty Parliaments, one after
another, and all in their Turns, to the irrefiftible Power of one grant Defpot :—In fhort, then
it would have been faid (and with great Appearance of Truth) that *divide, et impera* was
the minifterial Maxim ;—and that, what was
done,

done, or going to be done in *America*, was only the Omen and Prelude to the like fatal Eftablifhnents here in *Britain*. For the next Step would be (and upon a Pretence full as good, and altogether as conftitutional) to break to Pieces the united Force of the *Britifh* Parliament, by erecting one diminutive Affembly of States at *Edinburgh*, another at *York*, a third at *London*, and a fourth at *Bath*, or *Exeter*, or fomewhere in the Weft: And then, partly by flattering and cajoling,—partly by Bribes or Bullying,—by exciting their Hopes, or their Fears at one Time,—and their Jealoufies at another,—and by playing off each of thefe puny Affemblies againft its Rival, the Minifter would neceffarily become omnipotent;—and then farewell to the Liberties of *Old England*.

3dly. I object alfo againft all thofe of whatever Denomination, from the roaring Patriot in the Senate, to the miferable Scribbler in the Garret, who are the Penfioners of *France*, or *Spain*, or of any other rival Power: I fay, I object againft their being Judges in this Difpute, becaufe the very Intent of their receiving Pay is to promote Difcord, and to cherifh Faction;—and becaufe they cannot earn their Wages with more Facility, or with furer Succefs to their Employers, than by patronizing fuch Schemes, as will neceffarily keep up the Difputes between *Great-Britain* and her Colonies.

BUT

But here the Smartnefs of Debate (to ufe one of Mr. Burke's very fmart Expreffions) will be apt to fay, " Who are thofe Perfons againft " whom your Infinuations are levelled? Name " them, if you are able: And as you ought to " be furnifhed with the moft pofitive Proofs, " before you are intitled to throw out fuch In- " vectives, give them to the Public, in order " that we may hold thefe Traitors to their " Country in juft Abhorrence."

To all which ftrong Words I would beg Leave to fuggeft the following Anfwers.

1. I think it may be allowed, without injuring the Caufe of Truth, or even Charity, that a Man may be fully convinced of a bad Defign, or a wicked Scheme being in Agitation, without being able to prove, who are the Perfons concerned in it. It is not ufual for the Guilty to call upon the Innocent to ftep forwards and be their Accufers: Nor can it be expected, that the Names of the Confpirators fhould be the firft Thing in any Confpiracy which is to be brought to Light. Indeed, generally fpeaking, this is the laft Part of any Plot, or of any bad Defign, which can be fully known, or legally afcertained. And therefore, if either the Experience of former Times, or the Nature of the Cafe, can afford probable Reafons, and circumftantial Evidence in Support of this Affertion, *That there are Numbers of Penfioners to Foreign Powers*

*Powers now among us*—furely we have obtained all the Proofs that are neceffary at prefent towards eftablifhing a general Belief of the Fact, (which is the only Point here contended for;) and we muft leave to Time, that great Difcoverer of political Machinations, to unravel the reft.

WHEREFORE, 2dly. Let it be obferved, that the Hiftory of this very Country furnifhes us with ftriking Examples in Confirmation of the above Affertion. Particularly during the memorable Reigns of CHARLES the Second, and WILLIAM the Third, that is, juft before, and juft after the Revolution, there were many venal *Englifhmen*, both in the Senate and out of it, the Penfioners of *France*; who, to be fure, meant nothing by what they faid or did on thefe Occafions, and for fuch Pay, but the Good of their dear bleeding Country; who therefore ftormed and thundered, fpeechified and harangued, printed and publifhed out of pure, difinterefted Zeal for the Welfare of poor, *Old England!*

HENCE therefore I infer, 3dly. That the like may happen again, or rather has happened already, unlefs it can be fhewn, either, that *France* and *Spain* want no fuch Agents at prefent; or if they did, that they cannot now, as heretofore find them here in *Britain*. In regard to the firft of thefe Pofitions, whofoever will

will give himfelf the Trouble to examine coolly
and impartially into the flender Reafons alledged
on our Parts, for beginning two of the moft
bloody and deftructive Wars, that ever were
known, will find fufficient Caufe to believe,
that thofe Powers will always think it to be
more for their Interefts, to cut out Work at
Home for thefe reftlefs and turbulent Iflanders
(as they are pleafed to call us) than to let us be
at Peace among ourfelves, left that Circumftance
fhould give us an Opportunity of picking
Quarrels with our Neighbours. And moft certain it is, that both the former *Spanifh* (or the
*No-Search*) War, and the latter *French* (or the
*Acadia* and *Ohio*) War, were begun and carried
on principally with a View to promote the im-
mediate Interefts of the Northern Colonies; the
former to protect their Smugglers, when hovering about the Coafts, and when actually trading
in the prohibited Ports of the *Spanifh-Weft-
Indies*; and the latter, (a War, alas! begun,
without fo much as a Declaration of War!) to
do, I know not what! unlefs it was to enable
the grateful Colonies to rebel againft the Mother-Country, perhaps a Generation or two
fooner, than otherwife they would have done.
But be that as it may, one Thing is certain, and
beyond Difpute, that the more we are embroiled
among ourfelves, the lefs Caufe will the other
Powers of *Europe* have to fear our giving them
any

any Difturbance : And that 20,000l. or 30,000l. a Year fpent in Bribes and Penfions, properly difpofed, to raife an Oppofition againft Government, and to enflame the Populace againft their Rulers, will do more effectual Service to the Courts of *France* and *Spain*, than Thirty Times thefe Sums laid out in manning Fleets, or e-quipping Squadrons, or preparing and embarking Troops for an Invafion.

If therefore thefe Points are fo felf-evident, as not to be denied, the only Queftion now remaining is this, Can it be fuppofed, or is it credible, that a popular *Britifh* Senator, a *Britifh* Pamphleteer, or a *Britifh* News-writer, in an Age fo pure and uncorrupt as ours, would accept of a Bribe, or a Penfion on fuch difhonourable Conditions ? And are not all thefe illuftrious Perfonages either of fuch well-known independent Fortunes, or of fuch fpotlefs Characters, and approved Virtue, as to be fuperior to any Temptation of this Sort ? Now here I fay nothing, but chufe to be filent; and earneftly entreat every Reader to judge for himfelf. Indeed there was a Time, when a Text of facred Scripture might have been urged, as carrying fome Weight in deciding the prefent Queftion : " Beware of falfe Prophets, who come to " you in Sheep's Cloathing, but inwardly they " are ravening Wolves. Ye fhall know them " by their Fruits. Do Men gather Grapes of
" Thorns,

" Thorns, or Figs of Thistles? Even so every
" good Tree bringeth forth good Fruit; but a
" corrupt Tree bringeth forth evil Fruit. A
" good Tree cannot bring forth evil Fruit, nei-
" ther can a corrupt Tree bring forth good
" Fruit.—WHEREFORE BY THEIR FRUITS YE
" SHALL KNOW THEM." I say, there was a
Time, when the Authority of such a Caution
would have been regarded as more decisive than
the Productions of our modern licentious Presses.
But as we now live in very extraordinary Times,
full of new Lights, and new Discoveries, I for-
bear, left our Patriots should accuse me of Bi-
gotry, Priestcraft, or Superstition *.

---

* In the Year of the Rebellion 1745, and for many
Years afterwards, the *London Evening Post* (now a Republican) was then a flaming *Jacobite Paper:* During
which Period the Author of these Tracts had frequently the
Honour of being abused by him, under the Character of a
*low-church, fanatical, Oliverian Whig.* Once in particular
(above 20 Years ago) he was complimented in the high-
flown Strain of *Josiah ben Tucker ben Judas Iscariot.* The
Times are now greatly altered; and so is the Tone of the
Abuse. But the Author is perfectly resigned to these Vi-
cissitudes of human Affairs: And he has no other Favour
to ask of this, and of all his Brother Scribblers, whether
weekly or monthly, in Sheets, or in Pamphlets, than that
they would *never praise him*; because that, and that only,
he should look upon to be a *real Disgrace.* But it is not
the *London Evening Post* alone, who from a violent Jacobite
has commenced a fierce Republican. Many like Instances
may be recollected. And indeed the Transition is natural
enough; for if a Man can be so absurd as to think that there
is an *indefeasible* Right in any one Family, when that Family
becomes *extinct,* he turns a Republican.

4thly.

4thly. I exprefsly except againft all Perfons of *Republican* Principles for very obvious Reafons; for tho' they dignify themfelves by the Name of WHIGS, yet as they are not the genuine, *conftitutional Whigs* of this Kingdom, but an unnatural Superfœtation, and the avowed Enemies of the *Britifh* Conftitution, they ought not to be allowed to fit in Judgment in a *Britifh* Caufe. They are, it is well known, the profeffed Advocates for continuing and cementing the Union between *Great-Britain* and her Colonies; and yet they wifh, above all Things, to fee thefe Colonies totally exempt from, and independent of, the Power and Jurifdiction of the *Britifh* Legiflature. Now, how are we to reconcile thefe glaring Contradictions? And what is the Reafon for profeffing fuch a prepofterous Zeal for *America*, in Preference both to the Interefts, and Honour, of their native Country? The Reafon is this :--- They think, that by cherifhing and protecting a Republican Government in the Colonies, they are paving the Way for introducing a fimilar Eftablifhment into *Great-Britain*. Therefore *Republicifm* is the Bond of Union between thefe unnatural *Englifhmen* and their Fellow-Labourers of *America: Republicifm*, I fay, [pardon the Ufe of a new Word, where the Language doth not afford a better] is made the *common Caufe* for uniting Perfons of the moft difcordant Interefts, and different Inclinations in other Refpects.

C

And

And I will add, as an Illuftration of this Matter, and to fhew how far certain Perfons will go
to obtain their Ends, that the Republicans in
the Reigns of Charles II. James II. and
William III. joined the Conftitutionalifts in
bringing about the Revolution, chiefly with the
Hopes, that a Prince who owed his Election to
the Voice of the People, might the eafier be
dethroned by the fame People, whenever they
could get them into the Mood to do it, whether
with, or without a Caufe. For the very Sound
of Monarchy, however limited, or however well
adminiftered, is grating to their Ears. They
cannot bear to think, that one Man, or one Family fhould be fo much exalted above *themfelves*,
in Contradiction to their darling Maxim of a
natural Equality. And this Scheme for
laying the Foundation of a *new* and *equal* Republic is what the Republicans really intend by
ufing the Phrafe *Revolution-Principles* at this
Day. In fhort, we have now the moft authen-
tic Proofs, that their Predeceffors of old tried
all Means in their Power, and even applied to
the Court of *France* firft to prevent, and then to
defeat the Revolution, and to fet up a Republican Form in its ftead; alledging that it was
more for the Intereft of that Court to have a
Republican Government take Place in *England*,
fomewhat after the Example of that of *Holland*,
than any Kind of Monarchical Conftitution;
becaufe this, at one Time or other, might become

come a troublefome Neighbour, and a dangerous Rival; whereas nothing of that Kind was
to be feared from a mere fimple *Democracy*.
Moreover in fome Years afterwards, when the
Crown was fettled on the Houfe of *Hanover*, we
know it well, (for it is no Secret) that the Republicans both then, and fince, had no other
Merit towards that Houfe, notwithftanding all
their Boaftings, than that of referving its
Princes, like the Prifoners in POLYPHEMUS's
Den, *to be devoured the laft.* A mighty Favour
truly! For which our Ears are perpetually
dinned with a Repetition of the Services of
thefe Men towards the ungrateful Houfe of
*Hanover!*

AND now, my Lords and Gentlemen, having
excepted againft Courtiers and Placemen as *fuch*,
—againft pretended Patriots *on every Account*,—
againft the Penfioners of foreign Powers,—and
againft *rank Republicans*;---my humble Requeft
is, that the Caufe between Mr. BURKE and me
may be tried by the LANDED INTEREST ONLY.
*They* are certainly the propereft and moft unex-
ceptionable Judges; for they have *the moft at
Stake*; and their Intereft, and the Intereft of
the Public, muft neceffarily coincide. They
can gain nothing either by War, or Peace, by a
Submiffion to, or a Separation from, the Re-
volters in *North-America*, but what muft tend
to the general, as well as to their own particular

Advantage.

Advantage. Whereas almoſt every other Rank of Men may find their Account, in countenancing and ſupporting ſuch Meaſures, as may greatly enrich themſelves, tho' at the Expence of depopulating and impoveriſhing their native Country.

Nor, my Lords and Gentlemen, is this Cauſe beneath your ſolemn Notice and Regard. In the former *Spaniſh* [or no-ſearch] War, you ſpent above *Sixty Millions* Sterling, including the extraordinary Sums raiſed, and the freſh Debts contracted :---And in the laſt *French, Ohio,* or *Acadia* War, you ſpent above NINETY MILLIONS STERLING, if computed after the ſame Manner, viz. Additional Sums annually raiſed, and new Debts contracted. And all, alas! for what! ! ! ! *

BUT

---

* The late Dr. BUTLER, Biſhop of *Briſtol,* and afterwards of *Durham,* had a ſingular Notion reſpecting large Communities and public Bodies ; — a Notion which perhaps is not altogether unapplicable to the preſent Caſe. His Cuſtom was, when at *Briſtol,* to walk for Hours in his Garden in the darkeſt Night, which the Time of the Year could afford; and I had frequently the Honour to attend him. After walking ſome Time, he would ſtop ſuddenly, and aſk the Queſtion, " What Security is there againſt the " *Inſanity* of Individuals ? The Phyſicians know of none: " And as to Divines, we have no Data either from Scrip- " ture, or Reaſon to go upon relative to this Affair."— *True, my Lord, no Man has a Leaſe of h's Underſtanding, any more than of his Life. They are both in the Hands of the Sovereign Diſpoſer of all Things.* He would then take another Turn,

BUT without any Retrospect to Things past, let us look towards what is to come.

THE first Thing to be considered in the Dispute between Mr. BURKE and me, is, which of our Schemes *is the easiest to be executed, and the most practicable?* He proposes that all Concessions should be made on our Parts in Favour of the Colonies; but that none, or next to none, should be made by them in Favour of *Great-Britain.* Now this Proposal can never terminate the Dispute between us and them, but on one, or other of the following Suppositions.

FIRST, that the Parliament and People of *Great-Britain* are now convinced, that they have acted injuriously, illegally, and unconstitutionally in pretending to make any Laws, whether good or bad, to bind the *Americans :* Because they (the *Americans*) have their own Legislatures, which are totally independent of ours: And therefore we take Shame to ourselves by revoking these pretended, usurping Laws. For in short, the first Step in Politics, as well as in

---

Turn, and again stop short. " Why might not whole " Communities and public Bodies be seized with *Fits of* " *Infanity*, as well as Individuals?" *My Lord, I have* *never considered the Case, and can give no Opinion con* " Nothing but this Principle, that they are liable to I " nity, equally at least with private Persons, can account " for the major Part of those transactions, which we read " in History." I thought little of this observation the Bishop's at that Juncture: But I own I could not avoid thinking of it a great deal since, and applying it to many Cases.

Morals, towards fincere Repentance, is *Refti-
tution*. Or, fecondly, though we fhould not
give up the Point of *Right* of making Laws,
and cry *peccavimus*,—yet we take for granted,
that no improper Ufe will be made of the great
and manifold Conceffions, contained in Mr.
Burke's Scheme; becaufe we have to deal with
a People, who, (we know by long Experience)
may be trufted with every Thing, as being the
*Quinteffence of Honour and Honefty*, both in public and private Life, and particularly the *fair
unfullied Monuments of national Gratitude*.

Or if this likewife fhould prove to be a Pill
too large, and too naufeous for *Englifhmen* to
fwallow;—then, thirdly, we are to fuppofe, in
order to end all Controverfy, that the Trade
with thefe *North-Americans* is fo effential to our
Interefts, as a commercial Nation, that we muft
keep them in good Humour at any Rate, and at
any Expence;—left they fhould deprive us of
their Cuftom, to the utter Ruin of our Manufactures, Shipping, Navigation, &c. &c. &c.

Or laftly, we muft fuppofe, that *Old England*
is in Fact grown fo exceedingly weak and impo-
tent, and *America* fo very ftrong and powerful,
that it is in vain to refift any Encroachments,
which the Colonies may make on the Mother-
Country :---For in fuch Circumftances, it is
more prudent to fubmit to the prefent Evils,
great as they are, than to provoke our Conquerors to inflict ftill greater.                    I

I fay, one or other of thefe four Suppofitions muft neceffarily be made, before Mr. BURKE's Plan can terminate in real Peace, and reftore that Harmony, of which he makes fuch continual Boaftings. Let him therefore, at his own Leifure, take his Choice of either of the four, or even adopt them all, if he pleafes, and make the moft of them.

IN the mean while, deign, my Lords and Gentlemen, to caft your Eyes on my Plan (*childijh* as it is reprefented by him to be) of a *total Separation.* And firft of all, is it practicable in itfelf? And could it be executed with Eafe, if heartily fet about?---Suppofe therefore, that you were to recall your Fleets and Armies, and publifh to the *Americans* the following Manifefto, couched under the Form of an Act of Parliament.

" WHEREAS many of the *Britijh* Provinces,
" Colonies, and Plantations in *North America,*
" after having made, from Time to Time, va-
" rious Attempts to throw off, or fubvert the le-
" giflative Authority and Jurifdiction of *Great-*
" *Britain*, have at length proceeded to the
" greateft and moft daring Outrages for accom-
" plifhing the fame, by entering into illegal
" Combinations and traiterous Confpiracies, and
" even by breaking out into open and undif-
" guifed Rebellion : And whereas the Inhabi-
" tants in general of the faid Provinces, Colonies,

" nies, and Plantations fhew not the leaft Signs
" of Sorrow and Contrition for their paft
" Offences, nor any Defire to implore the Cle-
" mency of the Parent-State, which hath in
" all Inftances cherifhed, fupported, and pro-
" tected them at an immenfe Expence both of
" Blood, and Treafure; but on the contrary,
" continue to encreafe their hoftile Preparations
" for oppofing, by Violence and Force of Arms,
" the Execution of the Laws made by the fu-
" preme Legiflature of Parliament for the due
" Governance, and conftitutional Dependence
" of fuch fubordinate States and Provinces;
· " Be it therefore enacted by the King's moft
" excellent Majefty, by and with the Advice and
" Confent of the Lords Spiritual and Tempo-
" ral, and of the Commons of *Great-Britain* in
" Parliament affembled;---that every fuch Pro-
" vince, Colony, and Plantation which either
" now is, or at the        Day of        next
" enfuing fhall be found to be in Arms and
" Rebellion againft the Laws and Authority
" of the fupreme Legiflature of *Great-Britain*,
" fhall, from and after the Time above menti-
" oned, be totally cut off, fevered, and fepa-
" rated from the *Britifh* Empire; and that all
" its Inhabitants fhall be declared, and are here-
" by declared to have loft and forfeited all Pri-
" vileges and Advantages, Benefits and Pro-
" tection both by Sea and Land, belonging,
" or

" or fuppofed to belong to the Subjects of
" *Great-Britain*; and that they fhall be deemed,
" taken, and reputed, in all Courts of Law, and
" in all Refpects whatever, to be as much Aliens
" and Foreigners, and fubject to the fame Inca-
" pacities, as if they had been Aliens born.

" PROVIDED neverthelefs, and to the Intent,
" that as far as the Nature of the Cafe will ad-
" mit, the *Innocent* may not be involved in the
" Punifhment intended only for the *Guilty*; be
" it enacted by the Authority aforefaid, that it
" fhall and may be lawful for his Majefty, and
" for his Heirs and Succeffors, at any Time, to
" grant a Pardon to a whole State, Province,
" or Colony, now in Rebellion, under the Great
" Seal of the Realm; or to one or more Inha-
" bitant or Inhabitants thereof under the Seal
" Manual, and to *reftore* fuch Colony, or fuch
" Perfon or Perfons to their former Rights and
" Privileges, as *Britifh* Subjects, when it fhall
" appear to his Majefty in Council, that fuch a
" Province, or Colony, or fuch a Petitioner or
" Petitioners is, are, or fhall be deferving of his
" Royal Clemency and Favour."

SUPPOSE, I fay, fuch a Manifefto, or one to
this Effect, and couched under the Form of
an Act of Parliament, to be proclaimed to the
World concerning the Rebellion now exifting
in *America*: And then I afk, what poffible Difficulty could attend the Execution of it? Or

D                    who

who would even attempt to prevent it? The only People or Nation, who would wifh to obftruct the Execution of fuch a Law, are the *Americans* themfelves; for they have no Manner of Objection againft participating in all Kinds of *Benefits* to be derived from an *Union* with us; tho' they raife fuch terrible Outcries againft fharing in any of our *Burthens:* And yet their Efforts and Oppofition would be all in vain; becaufe, tho' you fhould even allow, that they are able to maintain their Independence in *America*, that Circumftance would not render them the Conquerors of *Great-Britain*, much lefs of the reft of the World, who muft of Courfe remain independent of them.

THEREFORE, fo far at leaft my Syftem muft have the Preference to Mr. BURKE's.

2dly. THE next Queftion is, *Which Syftem, can be carried into Execution with the leaft Expence?* And furely as we have hitherto been engaged in nothing but Profufion and Extravagance, it is now high Time to adopt, if we can, fome ufeful Scheme of Frugality and Œconomy in regard to *America*.

Now, my Lords and Gentlemen, here again permit me to afk, What Expences can poffibly attend the Execution of my Scheme?—The Thing itfelf is no fooner faid, than done. And all the Charges attending it are fummed up in the trifling Articles of Pen, Ink, Paper, and
Printing.

Printing. Whereas Mr. BURKE's Syftem, even according to his own Account, will entail upon you Expences always encreafing, nay, next to infinite. You muft, for Example, win over the Heads and Leaders of the new *American* Parliaments by Means of " Great Honours and " great Emoluments," [a pretty Periphrafis this to defcribe the Art of *Bribing !*] in order to cooperate with the Plans of the *Britifh* Parliament, and to bear a Share of the general Burthens of the *Britifh* Empire.

You muft alfo guard their Coafts at all Times, and protect them from all Invaders : And when they chufe to amufe themfelves by going *on fmuggling*, *trucking*, *huckftering*, and *buccaneering* Parties on the *Spanifh* Main, then you muft more particularly ftand up in their Defence, and infift on their Veffels not being fearched by the *Spanifh* Guarda-coftas. And if the *Spaniards* fhould think this an hard Meafure, and appeal to the Practice and Example of *Englifhmen* themfelves, who never fail to fearch the Ships of all Nations, if found hovering on their Coafts, you muft pofitively and vehemently fay, that the *Cafe is widely different* :---Then you have a fufficient Plea for declaring War againft them ;---then, my Lords and Gentlemen, refolve (as your Predeceffors did before) never to make Peace 'till the Right of Searching is given up ;—then fpend another *fixty* or *ninety* Millions in this new

D 2                                    Quarrel

Quarrel ;—and at laft make Peace (as they did)
without ever mentioning the Right of not being
fearched ; for which alone they pretended to go
to War.

But this is not all :—For when the Back-
Settlers in *America* fhall have " topped the *Apa-*
" *lachian* Mountains in fufficient Numbers to
" conftitute Hords of *Englifh* Tartars, pour-
" ing down an irrefiftible Cavalry on the un-
" fortified Frontiers ;"—who is to *refift* thefe
*Irrefiftibles ?*—Not the Colonifts or Provincials ;
for they, poor People, tho' now 150,000 ftrong,
[fee General Lee's Letter] to fight againft their
Protectors and Defenders, will neverthelefs be
fo frightened at the Sight of this *Apalachian*
Tartar Cavalry, that they will again cry. out for
Help to the Mother-Country ;—again, I fay,
as they did before, when only an handful of
* *French* and *Indians* appeared againft them.

---

* See, for a Proof of this Fact, Firft, A Meffage from
the General Affembly of *Maffachufet's Bay* to Governor
Shirley, 4th of *January*, 1754. Secondly, A Meffage
from the Council and Houfe of Reprefentatives of ditto to
ditto. Thirdly, An Addrefs from the Council of Reprefentatives of ditto to ditto. Fourthly, An Addrefs of the
Affembly of *Virginia* to the King. Fifthly, A Reprefenta-
tion of the Commiffioners met at *Albany*. And Sixthly,
Extracts from the Poceedings of the Congress at *Albany*,
all in the Year 1754. And all of them antecedent to the
Arrival of the two Regiments under General Brad-
dock. I would here recommend the Perufal of *The Controverfy between* Great-Britain *and her Colonies*, printed for
Almon, to thofe who wifh for a fuller Information on thefe
interefting Points; particularly from Page 107 to 136.

And :

And indeed, if the Mother-Country will act the
Part of *Don Quixote* to that Degree, as to ex-
pend her best Blood and Treasure in their
Cause, why should they incur any Dangers in
their own dear Persons ? Why be at the Pains
and Charges of defending themselves, when they
can so easily get the *British* Nation to fight, and
bleed, and do everyThing for them? Besides, Mr.
BURKE has already declared in express Terms,
[Page 98, 2d Edit.] that AMERICA MUST NOT
BE EXHAUSTED. Exhaust therefore yourselves,
my Lords and Gentlemen! as much as you
please, or as much as you can ; but do not
expect Assistance from *America*, even in her
own Defence, whilst she can get such Knight-
Errants as the *English* to fight her Battles ;
and whilst she can raise Patriots and Pamphleteers, News-Writers, and Republicans,
without Number, to yell the *American* War-
Hoop, and to denounce BLACK and BITTER
Days against those, who should even hesitate to
obey her Commands.

BUT the third Queston is, Which Scheme is
*best calculated to prevent the like Disturbances for
the future.*

AND here I would humbly beg Leave to obferve, that if my Scheme had nothing else to recommend it to your Notice, it most infallibly
cuts off all the present Causes of Dispute and
Contention between the two Countries ; so that
they

they never can revive again. Whereas Mr.
BURKE's is, at beft, but a temporary Ceffation
from Hoftilities; a mere Truce, 'till both Parties can be recruited, and better provided to
begin the War again. Nay, his would be found
in the Event,---not only to be no Manner of
Cure or Palliation of the prefent Evils, but even
greatly to foment them, and alfo to engender
many new ones.

For Example :---Granting, that Peace was
made on the very Terms, which Mr. BURKE
requires :---Granting, that we repealed every
Act of Parliament to which the *Americans* have
thought proper to object :---Granting alfo, that
we renounce for ever any Claim of Right
to levy Taxes :---And granting, in fhort, that
the *American* Affemblies became fo many diftinct
Parliaments, fupreme within themfelves, and
independent of all others :---Still, whilft thefe
*American Independents* are to be protected by the
*Britifh* Flag; whilft they are to enjoy all the
Rights and Privileges of natural-born *Britifh*
Subjects, both at Home, and Abroad, and in
every Part of the Globe,---Queftions *will*, and
*muft*, and *ought* to arife, on what Terms are
thefe independent *Americans* to be thus protected ? And what Compenfation is to be made to
the Mother-Country, for communicating to
them her moft valuable Rights and Privileges ?
Are they really to enjoy all Pofts of Honour and
Preferment,

Preferment, and all Places of Truft and Profit, and to be entitled to every Sort of Advantage, * Safeguard, and Protection, equally with the Natives of *Great-Britain*; and yet to make no Recompence or Acknowledgement for all thefe Favours?—The Anfwer of every ftaunch *American*, and of Mr. BURKE their Advocate General, muft be as follows, (for on their Principles they can return no other) That each independent *American* Parliament will be ready to *give* and to *grant* to *Great-Britain*, by Way of Recompence or Gratification, the whole Sum of—*whatever they fhall think proper, and no more†*. And that in refpect to the Regulations of *American* Commerce, they will confent, that you fhall put whatever nominal Reftraints you pleafe

---

* Where it not for the *Britifh* Fleets, and for the Fortreffes of *Gibraltar* and *Port-Mahon*,---and in fhort for the general Terror of the Britifh Name, all the piratical States of *Barbary* would immediately feize on *American* Ships, when carrying Fifh, or Rice, or any other *American* Produce South of Cape *Finiftere*, as their lawful Prey. And yet *America* doth not pay a fingle Shilling towards the Support of our Fleets, or the Maintenance of our Forts and Garrifons in any Part of the World.

† See the Refolutions of the grand Continental Congrefs, in Oppofition to the reconciliatory Propofal of Parliament for permitting each Province to tax itfelf, according to its own Mode. In thefe Refolutions they exprefsly declare, that they will be the fole Judges, not only of the *Mode* of raifing, but alfo of the Sum or Quantum to be raifed, and of the Application of it: And that the Parliament of *Great-Britain* hath no Right to decide as to either of thefe Points.

upon

upon it, provided you will not enforce fuch Reftraints by any Forfeitures or Penalties, which
fhall imply *the moft diftant Idea of * Taxation*;—
and provided alfo that, if Offences fhould be
fuppofed to be committed, they, (the *Americans*) and no others fhall be allowed to be
Judges both of the Nature, and of the Degree
of each Offence; and that the Caufe fhall be
tried no where elfe, but in their own *American*
Courts, and by their own *American* Juries.

Now, my Lords and Gentlemen, fuffer me I
befeech you, to appeal to your own good Senfe
and Underftandings on this Head.—Afk yourfelves this plain Queftion, Is fuch a Plan of
Reconciliation as Mr. BURKE propofes, a
likely Method of terminating the prefent Difputes between the Mother-Country and her Colonies? Nay afk farther;---Hath it fo much as
a Tendency to cool and moderate them? Or
rather doth it not feem much better contrived to
enflame, than to extinguifh; to kindle new Fires,
than to quench old ones?

BESIDES, when each of thefe *American* Affemblies fhall be erected into a diftinct Parliament,
fupreme within itfelf, and independent of the
reft,---Is it poffible to fuppofe, that no *new* Dif-

---

* The *Americans* have already declared, that they will
confider every *reftraining* or *compelling* Law, as a Tax upon
their Property.—See DICKINSON's Letters.

putes, or *new* Differences will arife between fuch
co-ordinate States and rival Powers ;---*neigh-
bouring, jealous*, and *contending* Powers, I fay,
whofe refpective Limits are in many Inftances
as yet undefined, if really definable ! And is it at
all confiftent with any Degree of common Senfe,
or daily Experience, to fuppofe that fuch Com-
buftibles as thefe will not fpeedily catch Fire ?---
Efpecially, if we take into the Account, the difcordant Tempers of the Inhabitants of thefe refpective Provinces, their inbred Hatreds and An-
tipathies againft each other, their different
Modes of Life, the Difference of Climate, Reli-
gion, Manners, Habits of Thinking, &c. &c.

Now, when Tumults and Diforders fhall arife
from any of thefe various Caufes,---What is to
be done ? And to whom, or to what common
Head, or general Umpire is the appellant Province to carry her Complaint ?---The Parliament
of *Great-Britain*, it feems, muft no longer inter-
fere; for that is no longer the fupreme Head of
the Empire, to which all the Parts ufed to be
fubordinate, and profeffed to be obedient;
therefore, being deftitute of any authoritative or
conftitutional Right to *compel* Submiffion, all it
can do, is to offer its good Services by Way of
Mediation; and that is, generally fpeaking,
juft nothing at all.

Is then the KING, (abftracted from the Parliament) to be appealed to in this arduous Affair?
And is he alone (in his mere *perfonal Capacity*)

E                                    to

to command the Peace to be preſerved between
State and State, or Province and Province.——
\* Is he, I ſay (abſtracted from being a King of
*Great-Britain*) to ſummon all the Parties before
himſelf and his Privy Council, in order to hear
their reſpective Allegations, and finally to deter-
mine, and ſettle the Differences between them?
Be it ſo : Then if he only is to decide, *as in an
Affair relating to his own private Patrimony, in*

---

\* The Princes of the Houſe of STUART took it into
their Heads to believe, that all Colonies were their private
Patrimony ; in reſpect of which the Parliament had no
Right to intermeddle. This Notion, ſo long ago juſtly ex-
ploded, is now revived, (ſtrange to tell !) even by modern
Patriots, and *American* Republicans : For they are the People at preſent, and not the King's Miniſters, who propoſe
to exalt the Prerogatives of the Crown to the Subverſion of
the Rights, Privileges, and Liberties of the *Britiſh* Parliament, and the *Britiſh* Nation. Indeed ſo far, it muſt be
owned, is Fact,—that as the Princes of that Houſe had the
firſt modelling of the Colonies, they introduced a Practice
(ſtill moſt abſurdly retained, tho' without any Power to enforce it) of bringing all Appeals before themſelves and
their Privy Councils, inſtead of before the Court of King's
Bench or the Houſe of Lords ; which is the only regular
and conſtitutional Mode of appealing, and the only one
now obſerved in Appeals from *Ireland*. However, notwithſtanding this *Impropriety*, as the King can ſend no
armed Forces to *America*, without Conſent of Parliament
firſt had for their Maintenance, and afterwards for autho-
rizing the Uſe of military Law, and military Diſcipline
among them, it may be juſtly averred, that the King doth
in no other excluſive Senſe govern *America*, than as the ſole
executive Power, which is to enforce and put in Motion
the Laws and Decrees of the ſupreme Legiſlature of *Great-
Britain*. See a very candid and impartial Account of this
Matter in a Book intituled, " Remarks on the principal
" Acts of the 13th Parliament of *Great-Britain*," from
Page 38 to 45.

*which*

*which we have no more Concern than we have with Hanover,*—it neceffarily follows, that he muft be invefted with fufficient Power (independent of, and without the Confent of Parliament) to enforce thefe Decifions; for a Decree without a Power to enforce it, and to compel Obedience, is altogether nugatory and vain.

Now, my Lords and Gentlemen, this brings us to the laft point of Comparifon between Mr. BURKE's, *and my Syftem,* viz. Which will leaft endanger, or rather, which is beft adapted to preferve our prefent happy Conftitution?

Mr. BURKE's you fee (if confiftent with itfelf) muft inveft the Prince with an amazing Degree of Power!---even with fuch a Degree as fhall be fufficient to controul the refractory States of A-merica, from one End of the Continent to the other. Nay, what is ftill more, this *fupreme, controuling* Power muft be the only CENTER OF UNION throughout the Empire. Nothing be-fides is fo much as propofed; and indeed no-thing befides (when the parliamentary Connec-tion is diffolved) can be fufficient to *tie* all the Parts together;---Parts fo widely diftant, fo to-tally disjoined from each other, as the *Britifh* Ifles and the *American* Continent.

Now here again permit me to afk, Is not this a very alarming Circumftance even in Contem-plation? And is all our boafted Zeal for Liberty to end at laft only in that *Union* and *Connection* which can be procured to the feveral detached

Parts of the Empire by Means of a Court, and of a ſtanding Army?---A large ſtanding Army to be kept up independently of the *Britiſh* Parliamént!-- And that too for the expreſs Purpoſe of enforcing the Decrees and Arbitrations of the Court!

But this is not all; for even a ſtanding Army would not be ſo formidable (becauſe it would ſoon moulder away) were no Means to be found out for its Support and Maintenance: Now this Scheme of many independent Parliaments points to the very Means of obtaining the neceſſary Supplies; for, as an ingenious Foreigner has very judiciouſly obſerved *, " A " Sovereign who depends, with regard to Sup- " plies, on ſeveral Aſſemblies, in Faſt depends " upon none. An Agent for the *American* Co- " lonies, [I ſuppoſe the Author meant Dr. " Franklin] in his Examination before the " Houſe of Commons, (*Anno* 1766, P. 122) " has even ſuggeſted in three Words the whole " Subſtance of what I have endeavoured to " prove on that Subjeſt; when he ſaid, *The* " *Granting Aids to the Crown is the only Means*

---

* See De Lolme's *Conſtitution of England*, the Note of Page 52. The Whole is a moſt excellent Treatiſe, and worthy the Peruſal of all thoſe *Engliſhmen*, who wiſh to underſtand, and to ſet a juſt Value on the diſtinguiſhing Excellencies of the *Engliſh* Conſtitution,---a Conſtitution, as he juſtly obſerves, the only one in its Kind, *ponderibus librata ſuis.*

" *the*

" *the Americans have of* RECOMMENDING THEM-
" SELVES TO THEIR SOVEREIGN.    Nothing
" therefore could be more fatal to *Englijh* Li-
" berty (and to *American* Liberty in the Iffue)
" than the Adoption of the Idea, cherifhed by
" the *Americans*, of having diftinct independent
" Affemblies of their own, who fhould treat im-
" mediately with the King, and grant him Sub-
" fidies, to the utter Annihilation of the Power
" of thofe antient, and hitherto fuccefsful Af-
" fertors of general Liberty, the *Britijh* Parlia-
" ment."

To thefe Reflections in this and in other
Parts of his Book, the judicious Author adds
many ftriking Examples, particularly the prefent
State of the Want of Liberty in *France* and
*Spain*, by way of confirming and corroborating
his Argument.    But in my humble Opinion
there is ftill a more forcible Example to be
drawn from the Cafe of the hereditary Dominions of the Houfe of *Auftria*.    For it is well
known, that the Princes of that Houfe rule in
as abfolute a Manner over every Part of their
vaft Poffeffions as the Sovereigns either of
*France* or *Spain*; and yet there are States (an-
fwering to our Parliaments) in almoft every
Country belonging to the *Auftrian* Dominions ;
nay, thefe States are frequently fummoned to
meet together ; which is not the Cafe with the
*general national Affemblies* of *France*, or with the

*Cortes*

*Cortes* of *Spain*.   How then comes it to pafs,---
that fuch Meetings produce little or no Effects
in regard to the obtaining of a *reafonable* Degree
of Liberty for the People, which every Subject,
if in his right Senfes, wifhes to obtain? The
Reafon is obvious :---There are a Multitude of
little States or Parliaments within the Territo-
ries of the Houfe of *Auftria* ;---the States of
*Auftria* (not to mention the feveral ftill leffer
States in the *Netherlands*) the States of *Bohemia*,
States of *Hungary*, of *Tranfilvania*, *Stiria*, *Carin-
thia*, *Carniola*, &c. &c.   But all thefe petty
States, or Parliaments being totally independent
of, and confequently *Competitors* with, and *Ri-
vals* to each other, never can act in Concert, or
purfue one general Plan, or attend to one *common Intereft* :---So that the Power of the Prince,
which would have been too weak to have contended with them all, if all had been UNITED
(like the Parliament of *Great-Britain*) in *one
compact*, *and general Body*,---becomes an *Over-
match* for any one of them fingly and disjointed
from the reft :---And this is the true Reafon,
why the Houfe of *Auftria* governs all her Provinces with fo high an Hand at this Day.   In
fhort, *Divide et impera*, explains the whole Myftery of this Affair :---And *Great-Britain* may
here fee her own Picture, drawn to the Life,
if ever fhe fhould confent to the Erection
of Parliaments in *North-America*, to be *co-ordinate*

*nate* with her own; and at the same Time
should allow these *North-Americans* to be *Co-
partners* with herself in one common Empire.

BUT why do I labour to prove this Point?
Mr. BURKE himself is as confcious, as I can be,
of the dreadful Effects, which muft neceffarily
attend the Execution of his Scheme. Hear him
therefore in his own Words:---* " We know
" that the Emulations of fuch Parties [to be
" created by the independent Parliaments of
" *North-America*] their Contradictions, their re-
" ciprocal Neceffities, their Hopes and their
" Fears, *muft* fend them all in their Turns to
" him who holds the BALANCE of the State.
" The Parties are the Gamefters, but Govern-
" ment keeps the Table, and is fure to be the
" Winner in the End. When this Game is
" played, I really think, it is more to be feared,
" that the [*American*] People will be exhaufted,
" than that Government will not be fupplied."

Now, my Lords and Gentlemen! be pleafed
to compare thefe *Fears* of Mr. BURKE, " that
" the *Americans* will be too *lavifh* in their
" Grants,---with the *Hopes* entertained by the
Agent (juft quoted from Monfieur De LOLME)
" that the *Americans* by Means of *liberal Grants*
" may recommend themfelves to the good

---

* See his Speech, *March* 22, 1775, fecond Edition
Octavo.

" Graces

" Graces of their Prince;"---and then you will have full Poffeffion of all Dr. FRANKLIN's favourite Speculation for removing the Seat of Empire from hence to *North-America*, and for abandoning the *Britifh* Ifles to the Care of Deputies, Vice Roys, and Lord Lieutenants. Many of you, I make no Doubt, have heard him declare, that the great Continent of *Britifh America* (which, according to his Computation, will contain nearly ONE HUNDRED MILLIONS of Inhabitants in little more than a Century) ought to become the Seat of general Empire. And it might be eafily gathered from the whole Turn of his Converfation, that he thought it no very difficult matter in the Courfe of Things to bring this important Point to bear;---that is, to induce fome future Sovereign of this Country to make the wifhed-for Exchange;---partly by the Obftacles which might be thrown in his Way, were he to perfift in remaining here [Obftacles, of which we have an *egregious Specimen* already] and partly by the alluring Temptations which might be offered him to quit this petty Spot, and refide in *America*.---I fay, many of you muft have heard Dr. FRANKLIN haranguing after this Sort; or have feen Letters from him to the fame Effect:---For that this was his darling Scheme, even before he came to refide in *England*, I have been well affured; as well as his favourite Topic ever afterwards. Therefore I will

will add, that by the Help of this Comment,
we can explain many Paffages in the Declara-
tions of the grand *American* Congrefs, which
otherwife muft appear to be either naufeous
Compliments, or grofs Contradictions:—The
Paffages I refer to, are the Proteftations fo
often and fo folemnly repeated, that they [the
*Americans*] have no Intention of feparating from
this Country; and that they have the pureft
Loyalty to the King, and the ftrongeft Attach-
ment to the illuftrious Houfe of *Hanover*. This
Key therefore unlocks the whole Myftery of
their (otherwife unaccountable) Proceedings.
And as POPE faid on another Occafion:

'Tis in the *ruling Paffion:* There alone,
The Wild are conftant, and the *Cunning* known.
This Clue, once found, unravels all the reft.
The Profpect clears, and CLODIO ftands confeft.

In the mean Time, becaufe his Majefty is gra-
cioufly difpofed to join with *Great-Britain* againft
*America* in this Conteft for Empire, (for in Fact
*that is* the *real* Difpute, whatever may be the
*Pretence)* not only many among the *Americans,*
but among *Englifhmen* themfelves, vent the
bittereft Reproaches againft him for being the
beft Friend and Protector of the Mother-
Country. Surely Pofterity will ftand amazed
at fuch a Procedure! The like Scenes of Infa-
tuation and Ingratitude (not to mention Difloy-

alty

alty and Rebellion) never yet difgraced the
Annals of the World! And it feems to be re-
ferved as a Mark of Infamy peculiar to the prefent Age, and our modern Race of Patriots, that
while the Prince on the Throne is inceffantly
endeavouring to keep his People free, and to
fecure their Freedom more and more by all proper and conftitutional Meafures, fuch Numbers
fhould be found amongft his Subjects, who are
equally induftrious to thwart his truly patriotic
Defigns, and to rufh headlong into Slavery.

BUT as Providence very often brings the
greateft Good out of the worft of Evils, let us
not defpair, but that thefe very Attempts,
wicked and unnatural as they are, may be the
Means of uniting all honeft, and well- intenti-
oned Men the firmer together, in order to fupport, and even to ftrengthen the prefent Conftitution. For Example, the two great Iflands of
*Britain* and *Ireland,* which are only feparated by
a narrow Sea, ought not to be feparated at all
by different Governments, Laws, or Parliaments. No good Reafon upon Earth can be
given for fuch a Separation: And it has long
been the ardent Wifh of every true Patriot in
both Nations, to fee them united. Indeed, the
beft that can be faid for the Continuance of the
prefent abfurd Syftem is, that the City of *Dublin* would be a Sufferer by the Removal of the
Court and Parliament :— I fay, this is the very
beft

Argument, which can be urged: And yet this has no Foundation at all, but in the Prejudices of the Populace, who are almoft perpetually miftaking their own Interefts. Even the City of *Dublin* would be a very great Gainer by fuch a Removal; for it would acquire *Induftry* in Exchange for *Idlenefs*; and then the Hands of its Tradefmen, by being the Hands of the Diligent, would enrich each other by reciprocal Employment;—the Hands, I fay, of thofe very Tradefmen, who in their prefent State, are almoft as poor, as the pooreft in the Kingdom.—That this is the natural and necefſary Courfe of Things, and not an idle Theory, or vifionary Speculation, I appeal to Faƈt and daily Experience;—and I appeal, not only to the Cafe of *Edinburgh*, which is now three Times, at leaſt, as rich and flourifhing, as when it was the Refidence of a Court, and of a Parliament; but I appeal alfo to almoſt every Town in *Ireland*: *Cork*, and *Belfaſt* for Example, have neither Courts, nor Parliaments; and yet their Merchants, Manufaƈturers, and Traders arc much richer in Proportion to their Numbers, than thofe of *Dublin*: And what is ſtill more extraordinary, thofe little Towns, which once thought themfelves happy in procuring Barracks to be ereƈted among them, in order to obtain, as they fondly imagined, *the Benefit of a great Flow of Money*, are now perfeƈtly convinced, that Towns

without

without Barracks, or Towns from which Barracks have been removed, are in a much more flourishing Condition, then those which have them.---Of so mischievous a Tendency is the Circulation of Money, when it becomes the Means of introducing Idlenefs, and of preventing Induftry. For, reafon as long as you will on the Subject, the actual State of Things will ever prove itfelf to be this, that Idlenefs is the Parent of Poverty, and Induftry the only Source of real Riches.

But, my Lords and Gentlemen, this is not all, and my Scheme of an Union with *Ireland* is calculated not only to introduce Wealth, and to prevent Idlenefs in the fingle City of *Dublin*; but alfo to diffufe conftitutional Strength and Firmnefs, and to create a Stability and Compactnefs throughout the whole Empire : Whereas Mr. BURKE's has as neceffary a Tendency to weaken and disjoin every Part of it, and to fow Jealoufies and Diffentions both at Home and Abroad, in the Mother-Country, and in the Colonies :--- The unavoidable Confequence of which would be at the laft, arbitrary and defpotic Power. In one Word, the true Motto for my Scheme is, *Vis unita fortior* ; and for his *Divide et impera*. Judge therefore, as Men who are more deeply concerned in preferving and improving the prefent Conftitution, than any Clafs of Men whatever;--judge, I fay, whether Mr. BURKE's Scheme

or

or mine, in regard to *America*, ought to have the
Preference. You have every Means of Information now at your Command: Your Birth, your
Rank, and Education, lift you up much above
the Prejudices of the Vulgar; whilft your patri-
monial Eftates and ample Fortunes fcreen you
from a Multitude of thofe Temptations, to which
other Men are grievoufly expofed. And yet, my
Lords and Gentlemen, let me tell you, that if
you will not exert yourfelves on this trying Occafion, in fome Degree proportionate to the Importance of the Caufe now before you, perhaps
it may never be in your Power to exert yourfelves
hereafter, when you will wifh moft ardently to
do it. Remember, therefore, I befeech you,
the Words the *emphatic*, and perhaps even the
*prophetic*, Words of a celebrated Partizan, whofe
Name I need not mention:—" Why, Gentle-
" men, will not you, who are *Men of great Land-*
" *ed Eftates*, take an active Part in the prefent
" Difputes? Your Neutrality, I do affure you,
" will not protect you. For if you will ftill re-
" main inactive at fuch a Crifis, what has hap-
" pened before, will happen again; and the
" *****'s and the *****'s who have but little to
" lofe, but may have much to get in the Times
" of general Confufion, will certainly become
" the great Men of this Nation."

*Fas eft et ab hofte doceri.*

INDEED the Eftates of the Church, we all
know, will fall the firft Sacrifice, fhould the
Republican

Republican Party now prevail. But neverthelefs, if you, my Lords and Gentlemen, fhould
be fo weak as to imagine, that Matters will
ftop there; and that your own large Poffeffions,
your fplendid Titles, your hereditary Honours,
and ample Privileges will efcape unhurt, amidft
that general *Wreck* of private Property, and
*Crufh* of Subordination, which will neceffarily
enfue; you will be woefully miftaken: — And I
muft beg Leave to fay, that you will have pro-
fited but very little, by what has been fo well
written in the Annals of this very Country, for
your Inftruction and Admonition.  For depend
upon it, the Ufe of *Committee-Men*, and the
Bufinefs of *Sequeftrators* are not yet forgot; depend upon it, I fay, that Ways and Means are
ftill to be found out, for the loweft of the People to get at the Poffeffion of the greateft of
your Eftates, as well in thefe, as in former Times.
Their Appetites are equally keen : — And if thefe
hungry Patriots fhould fucceed, after fuch an
Example is fet before your Eyes, who are you
to blame but yourfelves? — In one Word, you
know, or ought to know, that even the tender
Mercies of a Republic are cruel.  Or, if you are
not yet convinced of the Truth of this Affertion,
look abroad into the World; nay, look into what
is now doing by the Republican Congreffes in
*America*; and then fee how you would approve
fuch Men as thefe for your Masters.

HERE

HERE THEREFORE I willingly clofe the whole Difpute between Mr. BURKE and me: And I moft chearfully fubmit the Decifion of his important Queftion to thofe (but to *thofe only*) who are the beft qualified, the moft able, and the moft concerned to decide impartially. What therefore is to follow in this Treatife, is to be confidered rather *ex abundanti*, than as ftrictly neceffary for the Support of my Argument, and the Confutation of my Opponent. Yet, feeing that the following Points may ferve to elucidate fome of the former, and feeing that fo much has been faid, and fuch confident Boaftings have been uttered, concerning the Advantages, and even the Immenfity of the Colony-Trade; I will enter the more particularly into thefe Matters.

AND firft of all, and previous to any Enquiry into the Fact, I enter a folemn Proteft againft the difingenuous Artifice, fo often practifed by the Partizans of *America*, viz. That of BEGGING THE QUESTION. They beg the Queftion, when they take for granted, that if *America* were feparated from *Great-Britain*, all commercial Intercourfe would ceafe between the two Countries. For this is the very Point, which they ought to have proved, inftead of taking it for granted. And prove it they never can, 'till they fhall have firft demonftrated, that the *Americans* will no longer adhere to their own Intereft, when they

fhall

fhall be difunited from us. A difficult Tafk
this! In regard to which, they will find all the
World to be Unbelievers. Indeed I have already fo effectually filenced this Plea in my
Fourth Tract, from Page 203 to Page 220,
[2d Edit. printed for RIVINGTON, &c.] that I
hope I may be excufed from repeating the fame
Things. And as the Arguments there urged
have never been attempted to be anfwered, notwithftanding fo much Good-Will to do it, and
that my Opponents moft certainly would do it,
if they could, the natural Conclufion is, *that
they are* UNANSWERABLE.

THEREFORE I now enter upon the Subject
itfelf; and as the Trade to *Holland* and *Germany*
(and *more particularly to* Hanover) hath been
frequently reprefented as being very inconfiderable, and of fmall Importance; I have for this
very Reafon, felected this Trade from others, to
make it the Subject of our Comparifon with the
Trade to all the revolted Provinces of *North-
America.*

REMARK

An Account of the Value of the Exports from *England* to *Germany* and *Holland*; and also to those *North-American* Provinces, which are now under the Dominion of the Congress, for nine Years successively, viz. from *Christmas* 1763 to *Christmas* 1772, distinguishing each Country, and each Year.

| | From Christmas 1763 to Christmas 1764. | 1765. | 1766. | 1767. | 1768. | 1769. | 1770. | 1771. | 1772. | Total. |
|---|---|---|---|---|---|---|---|---|---|---|
| | Value of Exports. | Value of Exports. | Value of Exports. | Value of Exports. | Value of Exports. | Value of Exports. | Value of Exports. | Value of Exports. | Value of Exports. | Value of Exports. |
| | £. s. d. | £. s. d. | £. s. d. | £. s. d. | £. s. d. | £. s. d. | £. s. d. | £. s. d. | £. s. d. | £. s. d. |
| Germany | 1,164,335 3 9 | 1,869,465 18 8 | 1,811,268 2 3 | 1,506,293 10 11 | 1,490,733 9 4 | 1,138,866 9 8 | 1,372,569 0 4 | 1,318,490 2 4 | 1,154,181 6 0 | 14,233,283 13 9 |
| Holland | 2,048,467 9 9 | 2,026,778 18 11 | 1,809,904 0 7 | 1,550,709 18 0 | 1,744,974 2 2 | 1,656,551 13 1 | 1,766,333 10 2 | 1,885,397 16 0 | 1,897,805 1 4 | 16,060,942 17 6 |

Total of both Countries 30,294,226 11 3

## The REVOLTED PROVINCES of *North-America.*

| | From Christmas 1763 to Christmas 1764. | 1765. | 1766. | 1767. | 1768. | 1769. | 1770. | 1771. | 1772. | Total. |
|---|---|---|---|---|---|---|---|---|---|---|
| Carolina | 305,808 1 6 | 334,709 12 8 | 296,732 1 4 | 244,093 6 0 | 289,868 11 5 | 306,600 5 6 | 146,273 17 0 | 409,169 9 4 | 440,610 2 0 | 2,782,865 7 7 |
| New-England's four Provinces | 459,703 0 11 | 451,299 14 7 | 409,642 7 6 | 406,081 9 2 | 419,707 9 4 | 207,993 14 3 | 394,451 7 5 | 1,480,190 1 1 | 824,830 8 9 | 4,993,980 13 0 |
| New-York | 515,416 12 1 | 382,349 11 1 | 330,829 11 8 | 417,957 15 5 | 482,930 14 4 | 74,918 7 10 | 475,991 12 0 | 653,621 7 6 | 343,970 19 9 | 3,677,986 14 8 |
| Pensylvania | 435,191 14 0 | 363,368 17 3 | 327,314 3 3 | 371,830 8 10 | 432,107 17 4 | 199,909 17 11 | 134,881 15 5 | 728,744 19 10 | 507,909 14 0 | 3,501,259 10 0 |
| Virginia and Maryland | 555,391 10 6 | 383,224 13 0 | 372,548 16 1 | 437,608 2 6 | 475,954 6 2 | 428,361 15 1 | 717,782 17 3 | 920,326 3 8 | 791,910 13 1 | 5,104,030 17 5 |

Totals of the revolted Provinces 10,261,083 3 1

Superiority of the Value of the Exports to *Holland* and *Germany* over the Exports to the revolted Provinces of *America* £. 10,233,103 7 7

(To face Page 19.)

# R E M A R K  I.

ACCORDING to the above State of the Account, the Sum Total of the Value of the Exports to *Holland* and *Germany* alone, during a Period of nine Years, exceeded that to all the [prefent revolted] Provinces of *North-America*, by no lefs than 10,233,103*l*. 7*s*. 7*d*. which is more than ONE-THIRD of the Whole. And yet this very Period was more favourable to *American* Exports than any other: 1ft. Becaufe during this Period, there was the greateft Emigration from *Europe* to *America*, and particularly from *Holland* and *Germany*, that can be remembered; and each Emigrant, if a Cuftomer to *England*, whilft refident in *Europe*, not only fwells the *American* Account by his Removal, but alfo finks the *European*: So that he acts in a double Capacity, by adding Weight to one Scale, and by fubftracting, at leaft an equal, if not a greater, from the other: – 2dly, Becaufe During this Period, the Colonifts, and more efpecially the four *New-England* Governments, were preparing for a *Non-Importation* Syftem; and therefore were ftoring their Magazines with great Quantities of Goods to ferve for many Years. This Circumftance appears

G                                                on

on the very Face of the Account:—And 3dly, Becaufe the Bufinefs of Commercial PUFFING, during this Period, was carried, by the Parti- zans of *America*, to a greater Height than ever, in order to make the *American* Trade appear to be of much more confequence to this Nation, than it really is.—To explain this Artifice of Commercial *Puffing*, to fuch Perfons, who are not converfant in the Progrefs of Commercial Laws, I muft beg their Attention to the follow- ing fhort Narrative.—Formerly the Kings of *England* eftablifhed certain Duties or Taxes (generally five per Cent. *ad Valorem*) both on the Import and Export of Goods, *merely by Vir- tue of their own Prerogative*; and, as it was the *univerfal Practice* for every Prince to act in the fame Manner, thefe Duties or *cuftomary* Pay- ments were therefore called the CUSTOMS,---the Place where thefe Duties were paid, the *Cuftom- Houfe*, and the Officers who collected them the *Cuftom-Houfe* Officers. In Procefs of Time, the Subjects gained a little more Liberty; fo that the Duties which were originally impofed by Virtue of the mere Prerogative of the Crown, were af- terwards collected by the Authority of an *Act*, or *Acts* of the whole Legiflature.

AND yet, notwithftanding this Change of Au- thority, there was very little Alteration in the Syf- tem of Taxation: For *Exports* as well as *Imports* (in thofe Days of commercial Blindnefs) paid a
Duty

Duty of about five per Cent. * *ad Valorem*, as low
down as the Reigns of CHARLES II. and JAMES
II.—King WILLIAM was the firſt Prince who
had a true Notion of introducing wiſe and beneficial Regulations into the Syſtem of Exportation: For he cauſed the Duties to be taken off
from the Exports of *Engliſh* Woollen Manufactures, and of a few other Articles: Queen ANN
followed his good Example, and extended the
ſame politic Syſtem a little farther: But it was
reſerved to the Reign of GEORGE I. and to the
Adminiſtration of that *great* and *able* Miniſter,
Sir ROBERT WALPOLE (whom the Traders, and
the Populace always abuſed) to enrich this
Country by Means of a general Syſtem of *judicious* Taxes, and ſalutary commercial Regulations. For in one ſingle Act of Parliament in
the Year 1722, (8th of G. I. Chap. 15.) there
were about 196 Taxes repealed, [ſee CROUCH's
Book of Rates] Taxes which had been injudici-
ouſly laid, partly on Raw Materials coming in,

---

* Queen ELIZABETH ſometimes raiſed this Duty to 20
and 25 per Cent. by Orders and Warrants iſſued from her
Privy Council; that is, by her own ſole and abſolute Authority. Yet ſhe was *good Queen* BESS: And her Days were
*golden Days*. See alſo the ſhocking Number of Monopolies
granted in her Reign, ſet forth at large in TOWNSHEND's
*Collection*; or in Sir SIMON d'EWE's *Journal of Parliament*.
See more particularly the Debates which paſſed in the 43d
Year of her Reign, after a Struggle of upwards of 20 Years
for aboliſhing theſe Monopolies.

but

but chiefly on *British* Manufactures going out.
But tho' this excellent Law was productive of
the greateft Advantage to the Nation; yet it
muft be allowed, that like many other good
Things, it was the innocent Caufe of introducing fome Evil. For from that Time we may
date the Origin of our modern *Puffing*, refpecting the Export of Goods, which has fpread but
too generally ever fince. *English* Manufactures,
when entered in the Cuftom-Houfe for Exportation, now pay no Tax or Duty; therefore this
Circumftance becomes a Temptation to many
Perfons to make larger Entries for Exportation, than in Truth and Reality they ought to
do. Vanity, and the Defire of appearing to
be Men of large Dealings, and extenfive Cor-
refpondencies, and perhaps other Motives ftill
lefs juftifiable, will but too well account for
fuch Proceedings in the mercantile World.
Confequently in commercial Puffing, the Traders
to *Holland* and *Germany*, and the Traders to
*North-America* are much upon a Par: So that
were they to accufe each other, it might be faid
of both,

*Clodius accufat Machos, Catalina Cethegos.*

But neverthelefs in other Refpects there is a
wide Difference between them. For the Partizans of *America* are actuated not only by
Self-Intereft, or Vanity, but by Principles ftill
more

more powerful, viz. By fuch a Spirit of Enthu-
fiafm, and a Zeal bordering on Phrenzy, as will
ftick at nothing to promote the Good of the
Caufe. Hence therefore we may reafonably
infer, that tho' the Entries for Exportation to
every Country are fomewhat exaggerated, yet
that thofe to *North-America* are doubly fo.
Other Traders may probably confider thefe
puffing Advertifements [I mean their exaggerated Entries for Exportation] as a Kind of
Peccadillos, very allowable for the Promotion
of their Intereft; but an *American* Partizan views
them in a much higher Light, viz. as *meritorious*
*Acts done for the Good of his Country*.

REMARK

## R E M A R K  II.

AS we have been hitherto comparing the
Value of the *Exports* to the twelve *malcontent* Provinces of *North-America*, with the
Value of the Exports to *Holland* and *Germany*;
let us in the next Place confider alfo the Nature
of the *North-American Imports*, if compared
with thofe of other Countries.

Now all Imports may be divided into two
Claffes, viz. Raw Materials for the Employment of our own People, and taxable Objects
for the Purpofes of raifing a Revenue.

In regard to the firft of thefe,---if we fhould
caft our Eyes on the Imports from * *Ruffia* only,
will any one be fo hardy as to maintain, that the
Imports from *North-America* are at all on a Par
with them, in any Refpect whatever? Timber,
for

---

* A few fhallow, half-fighted Politicians have objected
to the Trade with *Ruffia*, becaufe the Balance, according
to their narrow Ideas, is vifibly againft us. But what Balance do they mean ?---Not the Balance of *Induftry*, for that
is plainly in our Favour; or, in other Words, we export
more *manufactured* Goods to *Ruffia*, than we receive from it.
And as to the Balance of *Money*, they ought to have known,
that it is much more beneficial to an induftrious, commercial Country to import Raw Materials *(if it wants them)*
than

for Example, Iron, Hemp, Flax and Flax-Seed, Linen-Yarn, Skins, and Furrs, Aſhes, Tallow, Hair, Briſtles, &c. &c.;—Can it be pretended, with any Appearance of Truth, that the Im-ports of theſe Articles (taking one with ano-ther) from *North America*, will bear any Com-pariſon with thoſe from *Ruſſia?* And yet, to the Shame and Diſgrace of an enlightened com-mercial State, ſeveral of theſe raw Materials are taxed, if imported from *Ruſſia*, in order to cre-ate a Monopoly to *North-America :* And others; when imported from *America*, are not only al-lowed to be entered Duty-free, which is juſt enough; but alſo have enjoyed for many Years the Benefit of large and munificent Bounties given by the Parliament of *Great-Britain.*—Given? To whom? To our non-repreſented Colonies: For it ſeems they will condeſcend to receive Bounties from us, tho' not repreſented, notwithſtanding they make this very Circum-ſtance a Plea or Pretence againſt bearing

---

than to import Gold and Silver ; becauſe there cannot be ſo many Hands employed in the manufacturing of theſe Metals, as in the working up of Timber, Iron, Hemp, Flax, &c. &c. to their reſpective Uſes. It is amazing, how little theſe ſelf evident Principles have been under-ſtood, or at leaſt attended to by commercial Writers of ſome Note and Character, and particularly by JOSIAH GEE ; according to whoſe Doctrine of the Balance of Trade, this Nation hath not been worth a ſingle Shilling for almoſt theſe 100 Years.

any

any Share in our Burdens. However all this is not fufficient to create that Monopoly in their Favour, which they, and their Adherents have long had in Contemplation. For the Imports of Raw-Materials from *Ruffia*, which are every Day encreafing, exceed thofe from *North-America* in Goodnefs, in Quantity, in Value, and in every Refpect, to a very great Degree.

But I forgot : " Pitch and Tar, and Indigo " are alfo Raw-Materials of very great Confe-" quence : And they are imported from *North-* " *America*, but not from *Ruffia*." True : Pitch and Tar, if imported from *Ruffia*, would have paid an high Duty ; but when brought from *America*, they receive a very large Bounty. And as to Indigo, had it not been for the many Hundred Thoufands of Pounds Sterling, which *Great-Britain* has granted in Bounties and Premiums to promote the Culture of this Article in the *Carolinas* and *Virginia*, [a tenth Part of which Sum would have ferved for the Cultivation of a better Sort on the Coaft of *Africa*] I fay, had it not been for this continual Foftering, and expenfive Nurfing, probably not an Ounce of it would have been raifed in *North-America*. And even as it is, the Indigo of *Carolina*, &c. is, generally fpeaking, of a Quality much inferior to that, which comes from other Countries. So much therefore as to Raw-Materials,—and let this fuffice in refpect to the great Returns

of

of our Colonies towards us, for making fo many
impolitic reftraining Laws againft ourfelves, and
for granting them fo many Monopolies, and
fuch extenfive Bounties.

THE next Head of Enquiry is, what *taxable
Objects* do we receive from *North-America*, if
compared with the Taxables of other Countries ? Mr. BURKE afferts Page 97, 2d Edit.
" That if *America* gives us *taxable Objects*, on
" which we lay our Duties here, and gives us at
" the fame Time, a Surplus by a foreign Sale
" of her Commodities to pay the Duties on
" thefe Objects which we tax at Home, *fhe has
" performed her Part to the* Britifh *Revenue.*"

WELL then, according to this Doctrine, we
are firft to fuppofe, that *North-America* fupplies
us with great Quantities of taxable Objects ;—
and fecondly that by fo doing, fhe hath performed her Part to the *Britifh* Revenue ; and therefore ought not to be obliged to contribute any
further. Now I am fo unhappy as to differ
from the patriotic Orator in both thefe refpects ;
that is, I firft deny his Premifes ;—and then
2dly, granting even his Premifes, I cannot admit of his Conclufion. Firft, then I do maintain, that *North-America* doth not fupply *Great-
Britain* with great Quantities of taxable Objects : For perhaps hardly any civilized Country in the World, of equal Extent, and under
the fame Parallels of Latitude, is fo barren in

H                          that

that Refpect, as *North-America*.—At prefent, I can recollect but two taxable Objects among all her Stores, viz. Rice and Tobacco. In refpect to Rice, I do allow that it hath been cuftomary to tax it; but as it is a Raw-Material, and an Article of Food, it ought never to have been taxed. And the Legiflature hath done wifely at prefent in repealing that Tax, which heretofore was laid on the home Confumption of it. The Fact is, that when Corn is dear, Rice becomes a good Succedaneum; but when the former is cheap, the latter will not be ufed in any Quantities here in *England*: For *Englifh* Stomachs will never prefer Rice to Wheat. In refpect to that Rice, which is carried to the reft of *Europe*, it ought to be remembered, that it pays no Duty at all, if exported South of Cape *Finifterre*. And as to the Duty which is retained on the Re-exportation of Rice to the Northward of Cape *Finiftere*, it is fo very trifling and inconfiderable, that it doth not deferve to be mentioned in a general and national View.

In regard to Tobacco; I admit it to be a very proper Object of Taxation. But here again, that which is re-exported pays but little Duty, if any at all. And with refpect to that which is ufed and confumed at Home, when the many Frauds attending it, together with the Expence of collecting are taken into the Account, the clear Balance will not be in any Degree, fo great as is vulgarly imagined.

BUT

BUT granting, that this Branch of the Revenue is confiderable, nay that it is *very* confiderable; yet there are a few unlucky Queftions to
be afked on this Head, which it will puzzle Mr.
BURKE and all his Adherents to anfwer in fuch
a Manner, as would do any Credit, or Service to
their Caufe. For Example; has the *Englifh* Legiflature done any Thing towards favouring this
*American* Tobacco-Trade, and raifing it up to its
prefent Height? Yes, it has; *England* has granted
a Monopoly to the *Americans* againft herfelf, by
feverely prohibiting, in feveral Acts of Parliament, the Cultivation of Tobacco in *England*:
So that at the worft, we have one Remedy ftill
in referve, viz. the taking off this Prohibition,
fhould the *Americans* be fo wrathfully-minded
as to refolve never to fell us any more Tobacco.
On this Ground therefore I ftill proceed; and
as the Friends of Mr. BURKE (if not he himfelf)
are fo very forward in exclaiming againft the Reftraints and Hardfhips, under which they pretend, that *America* has fo long groaned;—I afk,
why are they fo totally filent concerning the
many Reftraints and Difcouragements, which
*England* alfo hath long and patiently fuffered in
order to enrich *America?* And where is the
Candor, or Impartiality of fuch a Conduct?
Again,—if we have granted the *Americans* this
Monopoly, in order to encreafe their Trade, and
to caufe their Provinces to flourifh; what Effects

H 2                                              hath

hath it produced, in regard to the Sum Total of our own Revenue? And what is the Amount of the whole Duty on Tobacco? Is it equal to the Duties paid on the simple Article of Tea,—or of Wines and Brandies;---or in short of mere Fruit for our Mince-Pies, and Plumb-Puddings, for our Tables and Deserts? No, by no Means, it is not equal to any one of these *general* Articles: For the Duty paid on the Importation of Fruit alone greatly surpasses it. And yet we have granted no Monopolies, no Premiums, and no Bounties either to *China*, or to *France*, to *Spain*, *Portugal*, *Italy*, &c. &c. nor are these Countries, to which we have so vast a Trade, and from which we draw so great a Revenue, English Colonies.

But nevertheless, I will now suppose, contrary to all Proof and Matters of Fact, that the Revenue of the taxable Objects imported from *North-America*, was the greatest of all others;---what Inference is to be drawn from this Concession? And doth it at all follow from such Premises, that the *North-Americans* must, or ought to enjoy all the Privileges of *Englishmen*, without contributing any Thing towards the general Support, merely because we carry on an advantageous Trade with them, or have raised a Tax on their Commodities? Surely no: For by the same Rule, we must unite and incorporate with, we must protect and defend, the *Chi-*

*nese,*

*nefe*, the *French*, the *Spaniards*, *Portuguefe*, *Itali-ans*, &c. &c. for the fame Reafons, and on the fame Account. A Propofition this, which is too big with Nonfenfe and Abfurdity, to be feri-oufly maintained.

I will therefore difmifs the prefent Remark, with putting my Reader again in Mind, that let the Trade to *North-America* be what it may, of little Importance, or otherwife; it is a mere begging the Queftion, and a moft *difingenuous Artifice* to infinuate (as all the Advocates for *America* now do) that this Trade will be loft, if a Separation from the Colonies fhould enfue. On the contrary, it is much more probable, that, when all Parties fhall be left at full Liberty to do as they pleafe, our *North-American* Trade will rather be encreafed, than diminifhed by fuch a Meafure. Becaufe it is Freedom, and not Confinement, or Monopoly, which encreafes Trade. And fure I am that, on this Subject, Hiftory and paft Experience, as well as Reafon and Argument, are clearly on my Side.

REMARK

# R E M A R K  III.

THE Cafe of Emigrations from *Germany* and *Holland,* hath been in Part confidered already: But as the continual Emigrations from *Great-Britain* and *Ireland* (which I will always confider as *one* Country) have fomething more particularly prejudicial in their Nature; if compared with others, I hope the Reader will not think it loft Time, if I give them in this Place a diftinct Confideration.

A Set of Labourers, or Tradefmen refided lately in *Great-Britain,* or *Ireland;* and earned their Bread by the Sweat of their Brows. Their natural, or artificial Wants might be fummed up under the three great, and comprehenfive Articles of Food, Rayment, and Dwelling. In refpect to *Food,* including drinkables, as well as eatables, they paid for it by their Labour and Wages; and confequently were the Means of employing all thofe different Trades both in Town and Country, which were concerned in, or connected with, the raifing of Corn, or the rearing of Sheep and Cattle, the making of Bread, Butter, Cheefe, Malt, and Malt-Liquors, Cyder, &c. &c. alfo in the fattening, killing, dreffing, or preparing of Flefh, Fifh,

Fifh, Fowl, &c. &c. and in the raifing of all
Sorts of Garden-Stuff, and other Eatables:
The like might be obferved in regard to *Rayment*, traced from the Raw Material up to the
perfect Manufacture, and including every Arti-
ticle of Drefs, and all the Trades dependent on,
and fupported by it, throughout all its Stages:
*Dwelling* is the laft Article; in which Eftimate
ought to be included not only the original Materials for framing the Structure of the Houfe,
but alfo its fucceffive Repairs; together with all
Kinds of Houfehold Goods from the higheft to
the loweft Piece of Furniture, and their continual Wear and Tare.

THESE Perfons, who have been thus ufeful to
their Country, and have contributed to its Trade
and Riches, both by paying their own Rents
and Taxes, and alfo by enabling others to pay
theirs;— thefe Perfons I fay, have been in-
veigled away to leave this Country, and to fettle in *North-America.*—Here therefore I afk
this plain Queftion, What Recompence can
they poffibly make in *America,* for the Lofs
which hath been occafioned by their leaving
*England?* And what Gains will accrue to the
Mother-Country by this flourifhing State of her
Colonies? Begin therefore wherever you pleafe;
---examine, I befeech you this Matter to the Bottom, and mark the Confequences. *Food* for
Example, confifting of its various Kinds, and
including

including eatables as well as drinkables, *common Food*, I fay, muft certainly be raifed and manufactured on the Spot ; for a Man cannot wait for his Dinner 'till it comes from *England*. Similar Obfervations will likewife extend to the chief Part of every Article refpecting *Rayment* or Cloathing ;---not forgetting alfo *Houfing* and Furniture. For in all thefe Refpects, the principal Quantity, and the Bulk of the Goods, Manufactures, or Provifions muft be procured from adjacent Places, and not from a Country 3000 Miles off. Perhaps indeed a few, a very few Elegancies and Ornaments of Drefs or Furniture, or of the Dainties of the Table may ftill be imported from the Mother Country. But alas ! What are they, if compared with the Whole ? Perhaps they would not amount to more than a twentieth Part of the general Confumption.--- And moft certain it is, that if thefe Emigrants fhould not fettle near the Sea-Coafts of *America*, but wander higher up the Country for Hundreds of Miles, in purfuit of frefh *unpatented* Tracts of Land, (which moft New-comers are defirous of doing,) it would then not be a *fortieth* Part of what they would have either ufed, confumed, or worn, had they ftill remained Inhabitants of *Great-Britain* or *Ireland :* So little Caufe hath the Mother-Country to rejoice at this rapid Progrefs of the Population of her Colonies, arifing from, or caufed by, Emigrations.

But

But here, I know, it will be said, becaufe it hath very often been faid already, " That tho' " thefe Emigrants might not employ as many " Perfons. or mechanic Trades here at Home, " as they did before they left *England*; yet they " will employ more Shipping and Navigation, " and confequently more Sailors than hereto- " fore : And Sailors are the Defence, Sailors are " the Bulwark of the Nation," &c. &c. Now in order to detect this Fallacy, as well as the reft, I will here ftate a Cafe, which muft open People's Eyes, if any Thing can, refpecting even the Articles of Seamen, Shipping, and Navigation.

Suppose 1000 Tradefmen with their Families, Watch Makers for Inftance, fettled on one Spot fomewhere in the Neighbourhood of *London*, [I only mention *Watch-Makers*, becaufe it is computed, that about 1000 Families, or one third of the City of *Geneva* are fuppofed to be of that Profeffion.] Now the firft Thing which would attract our Notice refpecting Navigation, is to lay in a Provifion of Sea-Coals : And a yearly Supply of this Commodity for 1000 Families would employ a good deal of Shipping : Fifh would be the next Article, Sea-Fifh efpecially, whether frefh or Salt, in refpect to which a good many Sailors one Time or other muft be, or muft have been employed : After this, the like Obfervation will extend to Cyder, and to

I                      other

other Articles brought Coaft-wife; alfo to Wines, Brandies, Rum, Sugars, Fruits, Oils, &c. &c. imported from Abroad : Likewife to Timber of various Kinds for building or repairing, alfo for making a Variety of Houfhold Goods; to Iron, Hemp, Linen Cloth, and other Commodities, efpecially thofe of the bulky Kind: Now here I afk, Is it poffible to conceive, that, were this Group of Manufacturers to take Flight, like a Swarm of Bees, and fettle in fome of the Towns or Provinces of *North-America*, they either would, or could employ as many *Englifh* Seamen in their *new* Situations, as they do at prefent in their *old* ones ? And can any Man be fo abfurd as to maintain fuch a Paradox ? [Remember I limit the Matter to *Englifh* Seamen only ; for as to *Americans*, let their Number be what it may, *Great-Britain* never was advantaged by them. Not to mention, that feveral of the *American* Provinces have difputed, or rather denied, long before the prefent Difturbances began, the Right of preffing Sailors for the Navy; though it is well known, that this is the only Method whereby a Navy can be manned ; and though that eminent Whig, that upright, learned, and truly-patriotic Lawyer [Judge FOSTER] hath demonftratively proved in his Law-Tracts this Right to be as legally and conftitutionally vefted in the Crown, as any Right whatever.]

I

I will therefore take this Point relating to
Sailors for granted ; [at leaft 'till the contrary
fhall be proved,] and then it will follow, that
*Britifh* or *Irifh* Emigrations are to be confidered
as being very unfavourable to the Encreafe of
*Englifh* Sailors, as well as of *Englifh* Manufac-
turers; and that the Lofs and Detriment to the
Mother-Country are very great in both Refpects.

BUT here a Difficulty of another Kind, and
from a different Quarter, will probably arife.
It is this : — Granting that Emigrations are bad
Things in all Refpects ;—granting that they tend
to diminifh the Number of your Sailors, as well
as of your Manufacturers? yet how can you prevent this Evil ? And what Remedy do you pro-
pofe for curing the People of that Madnefs
which has feized them for Emigrations ?—I anfwer.---Even the Remedy which hath been fo
often, and all along propofed, *A total Separation from North-America.* For moft certain it is,
that as foon as fuch a Separation fhall take
Place, a Refidence in the Colonies will be no
longer a defirable Situation. Nay, it is much
more probable, that many of thofe who are already fettled there, will wifh to fly away, than
that others fhould covet to go to them. And
indeed we begin to find this Obfervation not a
little verified at prefent, a confiderable Re-emi-
gration (if I may ufe the Term) having already
taken Place. In fhort, when the *Englifh* Go-

vernment

vernment, which was the only Center of Union, and the only Bond of Peace, fhall be removed, Faction will rife up againft Faction, Congrefs againft Congrefs, and Colony againft Colony; and then the Southern Provinces will find to their Coft, that they have been egregioufly duped and bubbled by the Northern; then they will perceive, that they have no other Alternative, but either to fubmit to the tyrannical Ufurpations of thofe *canting, hypocritical Republicans*, whom they ufed both to hate and defpife; or elfe to implore that Help, Defence, and Protection of the Parent State, which they now fo wantonly and ungratefully reject and oppofe:—In either of thefe Situations, and under fuch Circumftances, there is no Reafon to fear, that many of our People will flock to *North-America*.

REMARK

# REMARK IV.

PREJUDICES and Prepoffeffions are ftub-
born Things in all Cafes; but in none
more peculiarly obftinate, than in relinquifhing
detached Parts of an unwieldy, extended Empire; there not being, I believe, a fingle Inftance in all Hiftory, of any Nation furrender-
ing a diftant Province voluntarily, and of free
Choice, notwithftanding it was greatly their Intereft to have done it. The *Englifh* in particular
have given remarkable Proofs of their Unwilling-
nefs in this Refpect. For tho' it was undeniably
their Intereft to have abandoned all the Provinces which they held in *France*, yet they never
gave up one of them, 'till they were compelled
to it by Force of Arms. *Now* indeed, and at
this Diftance of Time, we fee clearly, that our
Fore-Fathers were wretched Politicians in endeavouring to retain any one of the *French* Provinces, which, if it was a little one, would be a
continual Drain, and perhaps an encreafing Expence; and if it was a great one, might grow
up to be a Rival, and become the Seat of Empire. I fay, we can fee thefe Things clearly
enough at prefent: Yet alas! what Advantages
do we derive from this Difcovery? And what
Application

Application do we make of fuch hiftorical *Me-mentos* to the Bufinefs of the prefent Day? The remoteft of our Provinces in *France* were hardly 300 Miles diftant from our own Coafts; the neareft of thofe in *America* are about 3000. The Provinces in *France* were already fully peopled, and peopled for the moft Part by Inhabitants extremely well affected at that Time to the *Englifh* Government: Whereas the Deferts of *America* require firft to be peopled by Draughts either from ourfelves, or from our *European* Cuftomers; and then when thefe Emigrants have been fettled for a Generation or two, they become native *Americans*, who naturally forget the Supremacy of that Country, with whofe Government they have fo little Connections, from whofe Seat of Empire they are fo far dif-tant, whofe ruling Power they fo feldom feel (and therefore do not regard), and confequently whofe Claims they confider as fo many auda-cious Attempts to rob them of their beloved Independence.

But the Abfurdity of our prefent Conduct in not abandoning the *rebellious* Provinces of *North-America*, becomes ftill more glaring, when we confider farther, (what we now find by Experience to be true) that we can live and flourifh, even in our commercial Capa-city, without the Affiftance of thefe refrac-tory Colonies. For though it doth by no

Means

Means follow, that we should be destitute of their Trade, if each *American* Province was erected into a separate and independent State; nay, tho' the contrary hath been made to appear by such a Chain of Evidences, as no Man hitherto hath attempted to break or weaken, yet, granting the worst, granting even that these *North-Americans* traded with us as little after a Separation as they do at present, still it is possible that we may then live, because it is certain we do now live without them; and do not only live, but also enjoy as many of the Comforts and Elegancies, not to mention the Profusions and Luxuries of Life, as any Nation ever did, and more than we ourselves did heretofore.

THEREFORE (to be more particular on this Head, for surely it is a most important one) we were gravely told, that as soon as ever the *Americans* should shut their Ports against us, Famine to our Manufacturers, Bankruptcy to our Merchants, Destruction and Desolation to our Seaport Towns must inevitably ensue. Well, the *Americans* have now shut their Ports for a considerable Time against the Admission of *English* Manufactures. And what has ensued? Nothing, that I know of, so very dismal, or so very tragical; and none of those *black* and *bitter* Days, with which we are threatened, have yet appeared. Nay, according to the Accounts received from the principal manufacturing Places
and

and Diftricts throughout the Kingdom, it uni-
formerly appears that Trade was never brifker in
moft Articles ; and that it is not remarkably
dead in any :—Moreover it is likewife certain,
from the fame Accounts, that a much greater
Stagnation hath been frequently felt, even at
Times when every Port in *America* was open to
us, than is felt at prefent.

However, if thefe Partizans of *America*
fhould cavil at thefe Accounts, and difpute
their Authority, we have others yet to produce,
which furely muft carry Conviction (almoft in
Spite of Prejudice) as foon as they are perufed ;
[unlefs indeed it can be imagined, that the prefent wicked Miniftry have entered into a Plot
to charge themfelves Debtors to the Public for
almoft Two Hundred and Fifty-Five Thou-
sand Pounds Sterling *more than they received*,
merely to plague and confound the poor Patriots.]

The Account I am now going to lay before
the Reader, is the grofs Produce of the Excife for
the Year 1775, ending at the 5th of *July* laft,
compared with the like grofs Produce of the pre-
ceeding Year 1774, ending at the like Period.

|  | £. | s. | d. |
|---|---|---|---|
| Grofs Produce of the Year 1775, | 5,479,695 | 7 | 10 |
| Grofs Produce of the Year 1774, | 5,224,899 | 7 | 10¼ |
| Increafed Produce of the Year 1775, | 254,795 | 19 | 11¾ |

Now

Now it appears by the Particulars of the Account, that what chiefly caufed this great Increafe, was the greater Quantity made, confumed, or ufed of Low Wines and Spirits,— of the *London* Brewery,—of Malt, Hops, Cyder, and Coaches, in the Year 1775, ending at the 5th of *July*, than in the preceding Year. For as to feveral other Articles, there was a remarkable Deficiency, efpecially in the Excife on Tea, and on Liquors imported into the * Out-Ports; both which Branches, if put together, amount to no lefs than 79,380*l.* 13*s.* 9½*d.*— And yet, notwithftanding this great Lofs in two fuch capital Articles, the Produce of the others before mentioned fo much exceeded their ufual Income, that the whole Balance of the Year was, as I faid before, 254,795*l.* 19*s.* 11¾*d.* Now as our common People, our Artificers, and mechanic Tradefmen, our Journeymen, Day-Labourers, &c. &c. are the principal Confumers of, or Cuftomers for, thefe Articles (Coaches excepted) we may, and ought to pronounce, that thefe numerous Bodies of Men were not

---

* I am told, that this Deficiency of the Excife this Year, on Liquors imported into the Out-Ports, is owing to a new Species of Smuggling lately put in Practice, whereby the Revenue is grofsly defrauded. If fo, the Balance would have been ftill greater, had all the Duties on Rum, and other Liquors imported into the Out-Ports, been juftly and fairly paid ; or at leaft paid as fairly and juftly as ufual.

K                                in

in that ftarving Condition, (which it was fore-
told they fhould be) when they could fo much
exceed their ufual (and for the moft Part *unne-
ceffary*) Gratifications in Spirituous Liquors,
and Porter, Ale, ftrong Beer, and Cyder, as to
raife fuch a Surplus of Revenue. And in refpect to the Increafe in the Coach-Tax (which
was nearly 2000*l.*) furely this is a plain Proof
likewife, that our Merchants, principal Traders,
and Manufacturers (who were all to be infallibly
ruined) are not in that melancholly Situation, as
hath been foreboded of them by the *American*
falfe Prophets;—I fay, the Proof is plain, feeing that fo many new Carriages have been fet
up, inftead of the former being put down. And
I think, I may take for granted, that it is the
Trading, and not the Landed-Intereft, which
fets up moft new Carriages.

Upon the Whole therefore, and in whatever
Light things are confidered, it evidently appears
that we can have but little, or nothing to lofe;
but muft have a great deal to get, or (which is
the fame thing) much to fave, and many Dangers to efcape by a total Separation from the rebellious Provinces of *North-America*. The
Hiftory of all Nations, and of all Ages,—our
own Experience refpecting *France*,---the melancholly Situation at this Day of the once popu-
lous and flourifhing Kingdom of *Spain*,—the
prefent Demands of our Manufactures for Exportation,

·portation,---the State of Parties among us, and the ·Growth of republican Principles, all, all confpire to prove, that we ought to get rid of fuch an onerous, dangerous, and expenfive Connection as foon as poffible. In one Word, the longer the prefent Syftem is perfevered in, the worfe Things will neceffarily grow, and the riper for Deftruction ; it being morally impoffible that they fhould mend ; for the Fire, if even fmothered for the prefent, will break out again with frefh Violence ; and the found Parts of our Conftitution will be in great Danger of being tainted by the Gangrene of *American* Re-:publicifm.

POSTSCRIPT.

# POSTSCRIPT.

IN a Note at the Bottom of Page 52, (2d.
Edition) of my Letter to Mr. BURKE, I ex-
preffed myfelf in the following Manner : " The
" Inftances which Mr. BURKE has brought,
[at Pages 74 and 75 of his Speech, 2d. Edit. 8vo.]
" to prove that the Colonies, or rather that a
" few out of the many Colonies, have .been
" liberal in their Grants to *Great Britain*, dur-
" ing the Continuance of a privateering, fmug-
" gling, trucking, and huckftering *American*
" Sea-War, in which they were fure to be
" the greateft Gainers, fhall be particularly
" confidered in an enfuing Treatife, An Addrefs
" to the Landed Intereft of *Great-Britain* and
" *Ireland.*"

THE Minutes which I took at that Time relative to this Affair, and which I intended to
have inferted in the Body of this Treatife, were
the following, that the leading Men in the Government of the Province of *Maffachufets*, had,
fome Time before their famous Expedition a-
gainft *Cape Breton*, been guilty of certain Mal-
Practices in the Adminiftration of public Affairs, for which they were in Danger of being
called

called to an Account. That in order to divert the Storm, and to throw a Barrel to the Whale, they projected the Plan of an Expedition, knowing the Temper of the *Englifh*, and their Rage for Conquefts. Therefore, hearing that the Fortifications of *Cape Breton* were very ruinous, and the Garrifon both weak and mutinous for Want of Pay, Cloathing, and Provifions, they bent their Forces againft this Place. The Scheme fucceeded, and *Cape Breton* was yielded up; but the Joy of the *Englifh* Nation knew no Bounds : For the People, from the higheft to the loweft, were fo intoxicated with Notions of the Importance of this Port, [tho' now it is evident, that it is a very ufelefs one, if compared with others] that they forgot every other Idea in the general Tranfport; fo that the Planners and Conductors of the Expedition, inftead of their being called to an Account for their former Mifdemeanors, found themfelves careffed and applauded by the whole Nation; and to crown all, the Parliament itfelf voted a prodigious Sum of Money to reimburfe the *New-Englanders'* for their Expences and their Services in this glorious Work.

THIS, I fay, or to this Effect, was the Account which I received; - and which I believe in my own Mind, will be found to be for the moft Part very true, when it can be very thoroughly *examined into.* But as I have been hurried,

ried, by the *early* Meeting of Parliament, to
publish the present Treatise at least three
Months sooner than intended, I cannot at pre-
sent *authenticate* Facts and Dates in the Manner
I wish to do, in an Affair of such Importance.
Therefore I give this public Notice, that I build
nothing on the present Narration ; and I only
offer it (because not corroborated by sufficient
Evidence) as a probable Case, and as my own
Opinion.

INDEED I have a particular Reason for acting
in this cautious Manner ; seeing that I have
suffered already by making a Slip in an Affair of
this Nature, which in any other Cause or Controversy, would have been reckoned to be a very
*venial* one. The Case was this : In the First
Edition of my Fourth Tract, I had accused Dr.
FRANKLIN with having acted a very disingenu-
ous Part, in opposing and denying the Authority of the *British* Parliament, to lay a Tax [the
Stamp-Duty] on *America*, when he himself had
solicited to be employed as an Agent in the
Collection of that very Tax. In Letters which
passed between us, he denied the Charge, af-
serting first, that he did not make Interest for
a Place in the Stamp-Office, 'till the Bill was
passed into a Law ;—And 2dly. that the Place,
for which he asked, was not for himself, but for
a Friend, one Mr. HUGHES, who was accord-
ingly appointed by Mr. GRENVILLE. Now in
Con-

Confequence of this Information, I omitted in the next Edition, the whole Paragraph, and faid nothing, either *pro*, or *con*, particularly relative to Dr. FRANKLIN. And furely, every Thing confidered, and the *faux pas* of Dr. FRANKLIN concerning the *ftolen* Papers of Mr. WHEATLEY duly weighed, one would have thought, that I had made Satisfaction fully fufficient to almoft any Man in fuch a Cafe, whofe Pretenfions to *nice* Honour might have been much better founded than thofe of Dr. FRANKLIN. But it feems, I was miftaken: For before he left *England*, I was called on in Print, to make Reparation to his much injured Character: And in his Abfence, his Agents and Confederates, the Monthly Reviewers, have done the fame.

HERE therefore, I appeal to the Public, whether I have not advanced as far already in this Affair, as there was need for me to have done, fuppofing even (which is fuppofing a great deal) that every Thing which Dr. FRANKLIN faid was ftrictly true: For granting that he did not folicit for that Place in particular, yet it is a moft undeniable Fact, that at the very Inftant when he was declaiming at the Bar of the Houfe of Commons, againft the Authority of Parliament, he himfelf was an *American* Revenue Officer, in a very lucrative Poft, created by parliamentary Authority: He was a Poft-Mafter General in
*North-*

*North-America*; and the Tax, which he collected, and for which he was accountable, was an
*internal*, as well as *external* Tax. So that in
fhort, in every, or in any Light, his Conduct
was not of the fpotlefs Kind ; nor was my Ac-
cufation of Difingenuity againft him the lefs
true, whether he had folicited a Place in the
Stamp-Office, or not.

WHILE I am writing this,---a Paragraph, cut
out of a News-Paper, and dated from *Salifbury*,
*October* 15, is laid before me, which I am pofitively told, is reckoned to be UNANSWERABLE.
Now I have known fo many of thefe UNAN-
SWERABLES to fhrink to nothing, when examined
with any due Care and Attention, that I own I
am not much frightened at the Appearance of
this new *American* GOLIAH. However, let us
approach this formidable Champion a little
nearer.

 " THE *Americans*, fays the News-Writer, in
 " their Addreffes to the Public, urge as a Reafon
 " againft Parliamentary Taxation, the *great Dif-*
 " *advantages* they incur by fubmitting to fuch nu-
 " merous Reftrictions in Trade, which they deem a
 " Burden equal to, if not greater than Taxation:
 " And they alfo eftimate, that that Mode of con-
 " tributing to the Support of the *English* Na-
 " tion, is, upon the whole, more beneficial than
 " if they were to pay their Share by being e-
 " qually taxed with the Subjects of the Mother
 " Country:

" Country: But to be obliged to fubmit to
" thofe numerous Reftraints in Trade, and at
" the fame Time to be fubject to a parliamen-
" tary Taxation, they think is the higheft De-
" gree of Oppreffion.

" THE *Irifh* fubmit to parliamentary Re-
" ftraints in Trade ; but then, in return, they
" are exempted from Taxation. Why then
" fhould the *Americans* be burdened with both,
" in fimilar Circumftances ?"

HERE the whole Matter of Complaint is re-
duced to two Heads; Firft, That the *Americans* by being reftrained in their Trade, are
thereby in Effect taxed; and therefore ought
not be taxed a fecond Time :

AND 2dly, That this Hardfhip feems to be
the more oppreffive, becaufe the *Irifh* under fimilar Circumftances, are exempted from Taxation.

WITH refpect to the firft Head, it is a mere
*Begging of the Queftion.* For I have proved beyond Contradiction, that the *Americans* are not,
in *Fact* and *Reality*, reftrained either in their
Exports or Imports, except in a very few Articles ; and that they now enjoy the very beft
Market which *Europe* can afford, fee my 4th
Tract, Page 202---209. I have proved alfo,
that *Great-Britain* hath reftrained herfelf in Favour of *America* in Articles of at leaft as great
Value and Importance, as thofe in which fhe

L                         hath

hath reftrained *America* in Favour of *Great-Britain*. See more particularly my 3d Tract, Page 119,---121. Surely therefore thefe Things ought to have been taken into Confideration, and not to have been paffed over, as if they had never been mentioned : And it is exceedingly unfair and difingenuous to remember every Thing which makes on one Side of a Queftion, and to forget the reft.

2dly, With refpect to the other Head of Complaint, viz. That *Ireland* is exempted from Taxation, while fuch extraordinary Efforts are made for taxing *America*, I hope what follows will be as full an Anfwer to this Complaint, as what has been already given was to the former.

First therefore, I obferve, that with Refpect to the Claim of the legiflative Authority, which the Parent State makes over *Ireland* as well as *America*, both Countries are exactly on the fame Footing : See the 7th and 8th of Wm. III. C. 22, § 9. :—And alfo Lord Rockingham's Act itfelf, refpecting the Claims of the Mother-Country over *America* :—See likewife the Declaratory Act of 6. Geo. I. C. 5, refpecting *Ireland*.

2dly. The Mother-Country hath not only afferted, but maintained her Claims alike over both Countries, in the Affair of laying a general Poft-Tax on all Parts of the *Britifh* Empire ; fo that in this Refpect likewife both Countries are on a Par.                    But

BUT here I allow follows a wide Difference, which I will endeavour to account for, viz. The *British* Parliament never attempted to lay any internal Tax, except the Poſt Tax, on *Ireland*; whereas it is well known, that the *British* Parliament did attempt to lay an internal Tax on *America*.

Now to account for this *ſeeming* Partiality, I have the following Points to offer; and I intreat my Readers to attend particularly to them.

1. IRELAND never plunged us into any Wars ſince the Revolution; whereas *America* hath involved us in two, the moſt bloody and expenſive that ever this Nation experienced; the laſt of which brought on a Debt of 70,000,000l. Sterling, the Intereſt of which we are now paying.

2. IRELAND doth not drain us of any Sums of Money to ſupport and maintain its civil and military Eſtabliſhments; whereas *America* drains us for thoſe Purpoſes of upwards 300,000l. annually.

3. IRELAND drains us of no Money, by Way of *Bounty* on the Importation of her Goods, or natural Produce into this Kingdom; whereas *America* hath drained us of at leaſt 1,000,000l. Sterling for Bounties on Pitch and Tar, on Lumber, Indigo, &c. &c. within a few Years.

4. IRELAND is continually burthened with large Penfions, fome to Princes of the Blood, fome to other Perfons, and fome to flaming Patriots: For even Patriots will accept of Penfions if they can get them, and then exclaim moft bitterly—O Liberty, O my Country! Whereas *America* is totally free from this Species of Taxation, as far as I am able to trace the Matter.

MANY other Articles might have been enumerated, particularly the Reftraint formerly laid upon the *Irifh* fifhing on the Banks of *Newfoundland*, and taken off only the laft Seffion. But furely thefe are full enough; becaufe thefe, I hope, will fufficiently fhew, that there ought to be a wide Difference put on, every Principle of Equity and Juftice, between the Cafe of *Ireland* and that of *America*; and that the two Countries are by no Means in fimilar Circumftances.

WHAT is now to follow, is added at the Requeft of a foreign Nobleman, whofe good Senfe and Penetration led him to difcern, that a Crifis was certainly approaching, in which the Fate of this Country will be determined; and therefore wifhed to know, what was the Strength of each Party, and the Amount of the Forces on either Side.

A

A

# General Mufter of the Forces

### BOTH FOR AND AGAINST

## The Prefent Government.

PARTIES *for overturning the prefent Conftitution, and for fetting up fomething in its Stead, for which we have not yet a Name.*

1ft. THE Idle and Diffolute among the common People are for throwing the prefent Syftem into Anarchy and Confufion. They have ardently wifhed thefe many Years, for fome Kind of levelling Scheme whereby they might enrich themfelves at the Coft of their Mafters, and rob and plunder with Impunity. If Mr. WILKES, or any other modern Patriot can lead them into this Path of Glory, they will joyfully follow fuch a Leader, and become his devoted Fellow-Labourers, in the fame good Work; but if not, they will forfake him with as little Ceremony as they have done fome others, and look out for a new Leader.

2dly.

2dly. THAT Species among the *Whigs* which is properly *Republican*, is violently for a Change of Government, fuitable to fuch Principles; and thefe Men are now become of fome Confequence, not fo much on the Score of their Numbers, as on Account of their enthufiaftic Zeal, and of their breaking through every Tye of Honour, Honefty, and Confcience, for accomplifhing fuch Defigns. Moreover, as they put on every Difguife ; as they forge, lye, falfify ; as they ufe the Word Liberty merely as a Blind to conceal the Batteries they are erecting againft it ; and as they pretend to fupport and uphold the Conftitution, at the very Inftant they are planning a Scheme to deftroy it ; their Defigns are fo much the more dangerous by appearing to fight under the fame Banner with ourfelves ; and the Wounds they give, are the more difficult of Cure, becaufe they ftab and affaffinate under the Mafk of Friendfhip, and therefore take their Aim the better, and ftrike the deeper. In the former Plots and Confpiracies of the *Jacobites*, their Aim and Intent were to dethrone the reigning Family, and to replace another : The prefent Views of the Republicans, which they are inceffantly purfuing by various Means, and almoft contradictory Meafures, are, *to have no Throne at all.* Hence, by a Comparifon of the two Crimes, the Reader muft judge, which is the greateft, and the moft repugnant to the *Englifh* Conftitution.

3dly.

3dly. THE Advocates for making *North-America* independent of the *British* Parliament muſt, if confiſtent with themſelves, be for turning the *British* Conſtitution into ſomething very different from what it is at preſent, or ever was ; for the very Plea theſe Men uſe in regard to *North-America* is, that Repreſentation and Legiſlation (a very ſmall Part of which is the Power of raiſing Taxes) muſt always go together ; therefore as nineteen Parts in twenty of the People of *England*, and upwards of ninety-nine Parts in an Hundred of the People of *Scotland*, are not qualified to be *Voters*, nor ever were, *be their Property ever ſo great*, that is (according to this new-faſhioned Doctrine) are not repreſented in Parliament ; it muſt inevitably follow, that a vaſt Majority of the Inhabitants of *Great-Britain*, as well as *British America*, have a right to renounce their Allegiance to the preſent Government as ſoon as they pleaſe, and to ſet up for Independence. For in Fact, according to the dangerous Principles now openly avowed, all this Multitude of Non-Electors owe no Subjection to that Legiſlature, and to thoſe Powers, in the Choice or Continuance of which they were not conſulted. They ought not to be compelled to obey any Laws, which were made without their Conſent, or Privity ; and more eſpecially where they have no Repreſentation, they ought not to be ſubject to any Taxation.

Taxation. --So that being thus happily fet free from all Coercion of Government, all Reftraints of Law, and Burden of Taxes; and having learnt at laft to affert thofe inherent and unalienable Rights, which have been fo long ufurped, they are now reftored to a State of the moft perfect Freedom, and may either chufe another Form of Government, according to their own Fancy; or elfe live, as they can, without any Government at all. A bleffed Specimen this of *patriotic Liberty!* A moft comprehenfive Bill of Rights! fure of overturning, if carried into Execution, every Government, that either ever was, or ever can be, propofed to the World.

4thly. The honourable Society of the *Outs* will go as great Lengths to throw Things into Confufion as any Set of Men whatever; for as thefe Perfons have no other End in View than to get into Power, and to fhare the Emoluments of the State among themfelves and their Dependents, they will ftick at no Meafure, however unjuft and unconftitutional, to compafs this End: Nay, they will unfay the Things which they themfelves had faid in Adminiftration; they will blame thofe very Meafures which they themfelves had planned and recommended; and, in fhort, they will do any Thing, and every Thing, to raife the evil Spirit of Difcord and Diffention, to bring themfelves in.

*Laftly*.

*Laſtly.* THE Inconſtant and Diſappointed, thoſe who love to fiſh in troubled Waters, and thoſe who, having ſpent their Fortunes, have nothing to loſe, but may have a Chance to ſhare in the Property of other Men by a general Scramble; alſo the Deſperate and Daring of every Denomination; all theſe wiſh for ſome ſpeedy Change in the Conſtitution.

PARTIES *for preſerving the preſent Conſtitution, and for keeping every Thing in a quiet and peaceable Condition.*

1ſt. THE greateſt Part of the Nobility and Gentry of the Kingdom; that is, almoſt all thoſe who have the greateſt Property at Stake, and have the moſt to loſe.

2dly. A vaſt Majority of the richeſt Merchants, and principal Traders and Manufacturers throughout the Kingdom, are the warm Friends of Government: The Exceptions on this Head are few, and very inconſiderable.

3dly. THE Clergy of the eſtabliſhed Church are zealouſly attached to the preſent happy Conſtitution, wiſhing to preſerve, and to promote Peace on Earth, and Good-Will among Men: And in reſpect to the diſſenting Clergy, the moſt eminent and reſpectable (tho' it is to be feared, not the moſt numerous) act in the ſame

M                             laudable

laudable Manner, and endeavour to make their People truly fenfible of the many Bleffings they enjoy under the Reign of his prefent Majefty.

4thly. THE Proprietors and Stock-Holders in the public Funds will undoubtedly range on the Side of Government; becaufe they can get nothing, but muft neceffarily lofe by the Convulfions of the State, and by the Overthrow of that Conftitution, the Prefervation of which is their greateft Security.

5thly. THE whole Body of the learned Profeffion in the Law (Men who have acquired their Knowledge of the Conftitution from Authors of a Caft very different from bawling, difappointed Patriots, or hungry Pamphleteers;—thefe Men, I fay) in general agree, that each Member of the Houfe of Commons, tho' elected by one particular County, City, or Borough, doth not reprefent that particular County, City, or Borough, in any *exclufive* Senfe; for he reprefents the whole Commons of the Realm, one Part, and one Individual as well as another. A Member chofen *by* the County of *Middlefex* is not chofen *for* *Middlefex* exclufively, but for all the Subjects of the *Britifh* Empire; each of whom hath as conftitutional a Right to his Services, and may be as much affected by his particular Conduct, and therefore has as much Right to *inftruct* him, as any Freeholder in the County of *Midalefex*:

And

And he, on his Part, is bound by his Office to omit the *smaller* Interest of the County of *Middlesex*, or of the *Middlesex Electors*, when standing in Competition with the *greater* Interests of his Fellow Subjects in *America*, or other Places : — So that in short, tho' some few only, perhaps not a fortieth Part, of the Inhabitants of the whole Island, have legal Votes for Representatives, all in general, both within the Island, and without it, are *virtually* represented. That this is Fact and Law, that this ever was the Constitution of the *British* Empire, from the earliest Times down to the present Day, is such an apparent Truth, that it cannot be denied. Therefore in this Sense it is true, and in *no other*, that every Member of the commonWealth is supposed to give his previous Consent to the making of those Laws, which he is afterwards bound to obey, and to the imposing of those Taxes which he is obliged to pay. Indeed upon this Footing (viz. of virtual Representation in some Cases, and of actual Election in others) a free and well-poised Government can stand, and be supported; but it can be supported on no other :—Nay, the Government of the *Massachusets-Bay* itself, whenever this Colony shall become independent of the Mother-Country, must then, as well as now, be supported on this very Principle; that is to say, on the very Principle against which they

fa

so loudly clamour. And besides all this, the very same Reasons, which induce the non-represented Subjects in *England* to submit quietly and peaceably to the Payment of those Taxes, to which they have not given their Consent by actual Representation, ought to induce the *Americans* to acquiesce also; because, if the *American* Trade is so valuable, as reported, a *British* Parliament cannot injure this Trade by any Mode of Taxation, without injuring the Merchants, the Manufacturers, and the Traders in general of *Great-Britain*; and thereby sinking the Profits of their own Estates, and the Rents of their own Lands and Houses.

6thly. The whole legislative Power of the Kingdom will certainly support their own Authority, and not commit *Felo de se* to please their Enemies. They will not, they never can admit the Parliaments of *North-America* to be independent of them, or co-ordinate with themselves in the same State or Empire.

7thly. The whole executive Power of the Kingdom is at present in the Hands of his Majesty, and of those who act in his Name, and by his Authority. There the Constitution has placed it, and in no other Hands; nor is there the least Probability that mobbing, huzzaing, furious Speeches, and inflammatory Libels, without Arms, Artillery, or Ammunition, and
without

without a Treafury, will be able to wreft the executive Power out of the Hands of thofe who conftitutionally enjoy it.

AND now upon this General Review and Mufter of the Forces on the Malcontent, as well as the Government Side, let every one confider well within himfelf, what he ought to do at the prefent Crifis, as a conftitutional Patriot, an ho- neft *Englifhman*, a loyal Subject, and a prudent Man.

## THE END.

*Lately publifhed by the fame Author,*

## TRACTS Political and Commercial.

1. A Solution of .the important *Queftion, whether a poor Country, where raw Materials and Provifions are cheap, and Wages low, can fupplant the Trade of a rich manufaɛturing Country, where raw Materials and Provifions are dear, and the Price of Labour high.*

2. *The Cafe of going to War for the Sake of Trade confidered in a new Light.*

3. *A Letter from a Merchant in* London *to his Nephew in* America, *concerning the late and prefent Difturbances in the Colonies.*

4. *The true Intereft of* Great-Britain *fet forth in regard to the Colonies; and the only Means of living in Peace and Harmony with them.*

5. *The refpeɛtive Pleas and Arguments of the Mother Country and of the Colonies diftinɛtly fet forth; and the Impoffibility of a Compromife of Differences, or a mutual Conceffion of Rights plainly demonftrated; with a prefatory Epiftle to the Plenipotentiaries of the Congrefs.*

Printed for RIVINGTON, CADELL, and WALTER.

6. *A Letter to* EDMUND BURKE, *Efq; in Anfwer to his printed Speech of* March 22, 1775. ——*Printed for* CADELL.

## TRACTS Polemical and Theological.

1. *An Apology for the Church of* England, *as by Law eftablifhed, occafioned by a Petition to Parliament for abolifhing Subfcriptions.*

2. *Two Letters to the Rev. Dr,* KIPPIS: *Letter* 1ft. *Concerning the Extent of the Claim of the Church of* England

land *to regulate the* external *Behaviour of her own Members; and also to influence their* internal *Judgments in Controversies of Faith: Letter 2d. Wherein the Question is discussed, whether the* English *Reformers in the Reign of* EDWARD VI. *intended to establish the Doctrines of Predestination, Redemption, Grace, Justification, and Perseverance, in the Calvinistical Sense, as the Doctrines of the Church of* England.

3. *Religious Intolerance no Part of the General Plan either of the Mosaic or Christian Dispensation.*

4. *A brief and dispassionate View of the Difficulties respectively attending the Trinitarian, Arian, and Socinian Systems.*

To be published in the Courfe of the enfuing Winter.

*A Volume of select Sermons on interesting and important Subjects.*

All by the fame Author,

*9 7 8 3 3 3 7 3 0 6 0 9 0 *